DISCOVERING CHRIST

IN

THE SONG OF SOLOMON

DISCOVERING CHRIST
IN
THE SONG OF SOLOMON

Donald S. Fortner

 EVANGELICAL PRESS

EVANGELICAL PRESS
Faverdale North Industrial Estate, Darlington, DL3 0PH
England

Evangelical Press USA
P.O. Box 84, Auburn, MA 01501, USA

e-mail: sales@evangelicalpress.org

web: http://www.evangelicalpress.org

First published 2005

British Library Catologuing in Publication Data available

ISBN 085234-581-X

Scripture quotations in this publication are from the Authorised (King James) Version

Printed in the United States of America

To

FAITH

Her Daddy's Delight

Contents

1.

Why do we love him

Song of Solomon 1:1-4

'The song of songs, which is Solomon's. Let him kiss me with the kisses of his mouth: for thy love is better than wine. Because of the savour of thy good ointments thy name is as ointment poured forth, therefore do the virgins love thee. Draw me, we will run after thee: the king hath brought me into his chambers: we will be glad and rejoice in thee, we will remember thy love more than wine: the upright love thee.'

In many ways the Song of Solomon is the most precious and most refreshing of the Books of Inspiration. It is a book about fellowship and communion with Christ. It is not in any sense to be interpreted literally. It is spiritual. It is an allegory, a spiritual dialogue between Christ our heavenly Bridegroom and the church, his bride.

John Gill wrote, 'The whole Song is figurative and allegorical; expressing, in a variety of lively metaphors, the love, union, and communion between Christ and his church; setting forth the several different frames, cases, and circumstances of believers in this life.' There is no case, no circumstance, no spiritual condition that we may be in, regarding our relationship to Christ, which is not expressed in this sacred Song of Love.

C. H. Spurgeon said, 'This Book stands like the tree of life in the midst of the garden, and no man shall ever be able to pluck its fruit, and eat thereof, until first he has been brought by Christ past the sword of the cherubim, and led to rejoice in the love which hath delivered him from death. The Song of Solomon is only to be comprehended by men whose standing is within the veil. The outer court worshippers, and even those who only enter the court of the priests, think the Book a very strange one; but they who come very near Christ can often see in this Song of Solomon the only expression which their love to their Lord desires.'

In these opening verses of this 'song of songs' we see the cry of a renewed heart to Christ, the great Object of its love. These verses are not so much a description of our Lord as they are an expression of love to Christ and the desire of a renewed heart for his fellowship and some token of his love.

All who know the Lord Jesus Christ love him (1 Cor. 16:22; 1 John 4:19; John 21:17). A true, saving revelation and knowledge of Christ always creates an ardent love for him. To know him is to love him. It is not possible for a person to have a saving knowledge of Christ without a true heart of love for Christ. Anyone who does not love Christ truly, sincerely, and above all others, simply does not know him.

Communion

Here is the first thing that I want you to see. I hope that you can enter into it. The one thing all believers want is for Christ to manifest his love to their hearts in sweet, intimate communion. Our hearts' desire is expressed in the words of verse 2, 'Let him kiss me with the kisses of his mouth: for thy love is better than wine.'

The Song begins very abruptly, without any introduction. It opens with a cry of love to Christ, a desire for some manifestation of his love. It is the picture of a bride whose husband has been away for some time. But now she is anticipating his return. With hope, expectation, and delight she cries, 'Let him kiss me with the kisses of his mouth.' Oh, that our Redeemer might return to us and smother us with the kisses of his grace!

Jeremiah Burroughs once wrote, 'Permission to kiss the hand of a sovereign is considered an honour; but for that sovereign to give another the kisses of his mouth, is evidence of the tenderest affection, and is the highest possible honour.'

What we want is some fresh manifestation of our Saviour's love, some fresh evidence of his affection to us. Nothing could have been more delightful to the returning prodigal than the fact that his father ran to greet him and that, 'he fell on his neck and kissed him'. Nothing is sweeter or more precious to our souls than the kisses of mercy, love, and grace. Oh, that he might smother us with the kisses of his mouth! A kiss from the Saviour's mouth is a token of his deep love. A kiss from his mouth is an evidence of complete pardon, forgiveness, and acceptance. The ardent kisses of his mouth are so many evidences of his great love, deeply felt and freely bestowed.

We rejoice in his daily providence. We give thanks for his covenant mercy. We delight in his written Word. But what we ardently desire is for Christ himself to manifest himself to us by the gracious influences of his Spirit. We give thanks for his providence. We rest in his promises. We rejoice in his power. But we want his presence. We want him!

We long for Christ himself because we know by experience that his love is better than wine. Wine is a comforting, strengthening, exhilarating beverage. It rejoices the heart, revives the spirits, and soothes the nerves of a man. But the love of Christ is far better than the best of wine. When the love of Christ is shed abroad in our hearts by the Holy Spirit, it is like drinking some heavenly wine. Oh, that we might have this blessed intoxication that we might be filled with the wine of his love.

We rejoice in the knowledge of his love. It is without beginning. It is without change. It is without measure. It is without end. Electing Love! Redeeming Love! Saving Love! Preserving Love! Everlasting Love! Still, we long to taste his love in our daily experience. It revives languishing spirits. It comforts troubled hearts. It strengthens weak souls. It refreshes thirsty hearts.

If...

If the Lord is pleased to draw us by the cords of his love, we will
run after him. 'Draw me, we will run after thee' (v. 4). I hope we
recognize our need. We need Christ. We want him. We want him
to revive our hearts, enliven our souls, and quicken us. But I know
that he must do the work for us. We cannot revive ourselves.

Here is an acknowledgment and a prayer: 'Draw me.' We
acknowledge our own weakness and inability. Though we may
know our need and truly long for an awakening of our souls and
the reviving of our hearts, Christ alone can revive and awaken us.
We cannot work up a revival, or even pray it down. Revival does
not depend upon the actions of the church or the abilities of the
preacher. It is the work of Christ alone. Make this your prayer. If
you want him, so earnestly want him that your heart aches for a
manifestation of his love, pray like this: 'Draw me, O Lord, draw
me to thyself.'

How does Christ draw his people to himself? He draws us by
the gracious influence of his Spirit, by the manifestation of himself
through the Word of his gospel, and by the irresistible power of his
love.

If the Lord will draw us to himself, then we will follow him. If
he makes us know the constraint and attraction of his love, we will
run after him. Then no service will be too demanding. No obstacle
will be too hard. No sacrifice will be too great.

Knowledge

Our hearts burn with love for Christ because we know him. 'Because of the savour of thy good ointments thy name is as ointment
poured forth, therefore do the virgins love thee' (v. 3). I repeat
myself deliberately — If we truly know Christ by faith, if he has
been revealed in our hearts, we love him supremely. 'We love him
because he first loved us' (1 John 4:19). This is the true testimony

of every true believer. His love for us precedes our love for him. His love for us causes our love for him. But we do truly love him. His many attributes are to us a sweet smelling ointment. There is no aspect of his character, no attribute of his nature that is in the least measure repugnant to us. We love him because he is who he is. Believing sinners love Christ as he is revealed in the Scriptures (Ps. 45:1-9; Rev. 1:10-20). His holiness and his goodness, his justice and his mercy, his righteousness and his grace, his power and his tenderness, his immutability and his compassion, his wisdom and his sympathy, his wrath and his love, his judgement and his salvation, are all 'good ointments' in the estimation of our souls.

We have looked him over from every point of view, as the Holy Spirit has revealed him to us, and this is our conclusion: 'He is altogether lovely.' There is not one attribute, not one word, not one act of our Lord that does not enhance his beauty to our hearts. In his humiliation, in his life, in his death, in his resurrection, in his exaltation, in his majestic sovereignty, in his glorious coming, in his strict judgement, and in his everlasting glory — 'He is altogether lovely!'

His Name, by which he has revealed himself, is like an enchanting perfume to our souls. 'The virgins', those who have been made pure by him, love the Lord because of his Name. His Name is Immanuel — 'God with us.' His Name is Jesus — 'Jah-Hosea'; 'Divine Saviour'. His Name is Christ — 'God's anointed'. His Name is 'The LORD our Righteousness'.

In the eyes of others our adorable Saviour has no form nor comeliness for which they might desire him. But in the eyes of his own he is truly precious. He is fairer than ten thousand. In comparison with him, all others must be despised. We are made to cry, 'Whom have I in heaven but thee? And there is none upon earth I desire beside thee.'

Charles Simeon said of Christ's church and bride: 'She is altogether occupied with the savour of her Beloved's name, the perfume of which makes *every* other odour worthless at least, if not nauseous and offensive. In a word, so entirely does this beloved

Object fill her soul, that with him a dungeon would be heaven; and without him, heaven itself would be a dungeon.'

Rejoice

I do not know what the Lord may be pleased to do for us in this day. In the midst of wrath, I pray that he will remember mercy, that he will revive his work. It is my earnest hope, it is the burden of my heart, it is the cry of my soul that he may be pleased to send us a mighty awakening. I pray that he will reveal himself in our midst. Yet, whatever he does, or does not do, we must, even in our times of spiritual emptiness and barrenness, rejoice in our Saviour and in his love. 'The king hath brought me into his chambers: we will be glad and rejoice in thee, we will remember thy love more than wine: the upright love thee' (v. 4).

We must not despise the grace he has bestowed upon us. We must not murmur against his providence. When he speaks and when he is silent, when he sends refreshing and when he sends barrenness, when he reveals himself and when he hides himself, let us rejoice in the Lord. We have abundant reason to rejoice and be glad.

Christ has accepted us as his own. The King has brought us into his chambers! Let us ever remember his love. We have many proofs of it. He may for a time hide his face from us, but he loves us still. Even now, though our hearts may seem dull and heavy, we love the Lord our Redeemer. We will wait before him in loving submission. Whatever he is pleased to do, we will love him. We have reason enough to do so, who can say, 'My beloved is mine, and I am his!'

2.

Four characteristics of true faith

Song of Solomon 1:5-7

'I am black, but comely, O ye daughters of Jerusalem, as the tents of Kedar, as the curtains of Solomon. Look not upon me, because I am black, because the sun hath looked upon me: my mother's children were angry with me; they made me the keeper of the vineyards; but mine own vineyard have I not kept. Tell me, O thou whom my soul loveth, where thou feedest, where thou makest thy flock to rest at noon: for why should I be as one that turneth aside by the flocks of thy companions?'

Here is a beautiful picture of true faith. It expresses every believer's thoughts concerning himself and his Saviour. In verses 5 and 6, the church, the Bride of Christ, speaks about herself to the daughters of Jerusalem:

> I am black, but comely, O ye daughters of Jerusalem, as the tents of Kedar, as the curtains of Solomon. Look not upon me, because I am black, because the sun hath looked upon me: my mother's children were angry with me; they made me the keeper of the vineyards; but mine own vineyard have I not kept.

Then, in verse 7, she speaks about herself to her Beloved Lord. 'Tell me, O thou whom my soul loveth, where thou feedest, where thou makest thy flock to rest at noon: for why should I be as one that turneth aside by the flocks of thy companions?'

'Black'

True faith acknowledges and confesses sin. 'I am black.' The people of God are charged by both the world and by self-righteous religionists with many evils. But none of our enemies have such a loathsome view of us as we have of ourselves. Do any charge us with evil? It is true. 'I am black…My own vineyard have I not kept.' I am black in myself, by nature. I am black in the eyes of others, because of my actions. I am black in my own eyes. True faith does not defend itself. It does not seek any excuse for sin. True faith acknowledges and confesses sin (Job 40:3-5; 42:5-6; Ps. 51:4-5).

The believer is a person with two distinct natures, the flesh and the spirit. These two natures are constantly at war with one another, so long as we live in this world (Rom. 7:14-24; Gal. 5:17).

We are sinners by nature. We are sinners by choice. We are sinners by practice. We are sinners at heart. Sin is not to be measured by our actions, but by our attitude. Sin is not to be measured by our deeds, but by our principles. Sin is not so much what we do, but what we are. Sin is mixed with all we do. Old man Adam is still present with us. He is no longer master, but he is still present. That is a fact from which we cannot escape.

Yes, we do love Christ. He has created in us true love for himself. But before you were converted, did you ever think that you could love God so little as you do? — We do pray. Grace has taught every believing heart to pray. But before God saved you, did you ever think that prayer could be so difficult as it actually is? — We bow to and trust God's wise, unerring providence. But before God gave you faith in Christ, did you ever think that a believer could grumble so much against the providence of God as you do? Did you ever think that a believer could be so unbelieving? — Thank God, he has set our hearts on things above. But before God revealed himself to you and in you in Christ, did you ever think that a person who knows the Lord could be so thoroughly attached to the toys of this world as you are? We are his witnesses. We confess Christ before men. But before you knew the Lord, did you ever think that a believer could be so reluctant and timid about holding up the banner of Christ among his enemies as you are?

Sin is so much a part of us that it is mixed with all we do and all we are. We despise that fact, but we cannot, in honesty, deny it (1 John 1:10). Truly, we confess, 'I am black.'

'Comely'

True faith acknowledges and confesses sin while resting upon the merits of Christ alone. In ourselves we are black, but in Christ we are comely (suitable, beautiful, seemly). In our own eyes we are black, but in the eyes of God we are comely (S. of S. 4:1; Ezek. 16:9-14).

The Lord Jesus Christ has made us beautiful in the eyes of God through his righteousness and shed blood; and we trust his merits alone for our acceptance with God. Be sure that you understand this. In Christ every true believer is perfect and complete (Col. 2:10; 1:28). 'He was manifest to take away our sin; and in him is no sin!' Though full of sin in ourselves, in him we have no sin (1 John 3:5). Through the merits of his own blood and righteousness, the Lord Jesus Christ will present us before the Father in the perfection of holiness (Eph. 5:25-27).

All who are born of God trust the merits of the Lord Jesus Christ alone for their entire, complete, absolute, and everlasting acceptance with God. We are nothing. We have nothing. We can do nothing in ourselves and by ourselves that God can or will accept. All our hope before God is in Christ (Lam. 3:22-26; 1 Cor. 1:30). He is our only Wisdom, Righteousness, Sanctification, and Redemption. That means he is our only hope before God.

Loves

True faith acknowledges and confesses sin while looking to Christ alone for acceptance with God. And true faith loves Christ supremely. The Lord Jesus Christ is our Beloved. He is that One who is loved by all who trust him. It is written, 'If any man love not the Lord Jesus Christ, let him be Anathema Maranatha' (1 Cor. 16:22). All believers love the Son of God.

Notice the title that is here given to our Lord, 'Tell me, O thou whom my soul loveth.' This is every believer's humble, but honest acknowledgement: 'We love him because he first loved us' (1 John 4:19). His love for us precedes our love for him. His love for us is infinitely greater than our love to him. His love for us is the cause of our love to him. But if we know the Lord Jesus Christ, we love him.

Our love for Christ is something the world can never understand, because they do not know our Lord (1 John 3:1-2). We love him because of all that he has done for us. We love him because of all that he has given us. We love him because of himself, because he is who he is. And we love him supremely (Matt. 10:37-39). Our love for Christ grows as our knowledge of him grows. Our love for Christ is the motive of our actions (2 Cor. 5:14). Our love for Christ is the governing principle of our lives.

Even Peter, in the teeth of his horrible sin, honestly and truthfully confessed, 'Thou knowest that I love thee.' Like Peter, we err greatly, fall often, and act presumptuously. But, like Peter, every true believer, at the very core of his being, loves Christ.

Does this seem confusing? It really shouldn't. If we would learn to quit playing religion and be honest with ourselves and honest with God, we would acknowledge these things. A man who truly loves his wife, a truly faithful husband, often acts as though he does not love her at all. A woman who truly loves her husband, one who is a faithful wife often acts as though she does not love him at all. No one else may perceive it, but ask the man or the woman and they will tell you it is so with weeping eyes and broken heart.

So it is with God's saints in this world. We love our Saviour. We seek to serve him and honour him in all things. Yet, we often think, and say, and do things that are totally contrary to that love. Yet, with Peter, with weeping eyes and broken hearts, we confess, 'Lord, thou knowest all things, thou knowest that I love thee.'

Seeks

True faith seeks Christ continually. This is what we see in verse 7: 'Tell me, O thou whom my soul loveth, where thou feedest, where thou makest thy flock to rest at noon: for why should I be as one that turneth aside by the flocks of thy companions?'

True faith is never self-confident and self-sufficient. It continually seeks Christ (Heb. 12:1-4; Phil. 3:7-14). Faith is not only an act of life. Faith is a way of life. We seek him, not just what we might hope to get from him. We seek him because we need him, because we know we must have him. We seek him earnestly, continually, in the place where he has promised he will be found, in his Word, in his house, among his people. And we seek him with this confidence: All who truly seek him shall find him (Jer. 29:10-13).

Let us never seek to grow beyond simple, childlike faith in the Lord Jesus Christ. 'As ye have therefore received Christ Jesus the Lord, so walk ye in him' (Col. 2:6). This is the only way we can walk with him. We must ever seek him and walk with him as sinners needing to be bathed in his blood, robed in his righteousness, and saved by his grace. May God give us the grace to do so.

3.

The footsteps of the flock

Song of Solomon 1:7-11

'Tell me, O thou whom my soul loveth, where thou feedest, where thou makest thy flock to rest at noon: for why should I be as one that turneth aside by the flocks of thy companions? If thou know not, O thou fairest among women, go thy way forth by the footsteps of the flock, and feed thy kids beside the shepherds' tents. I have compared thee, O my love, to a company of horses in Pharaoh's chariots. Thy cheeks are comely with rows of jewels, thy neck with chains of gold. We will make thee borders of gold with studs of silver.'

I direct your attention to just three things in these verses. These three things ought to be matters of great concern to all who read these lines:

1. A question asked

In verse 7 a question is asked. Here it is the bride, the church, speaking to him whom her soul loves, the Lord Jesus Christ. Every word, every syllable of this question is worthy of our careful meditation. 'Tell me, O thou whom my soul loveth, where thou feedest, where thou makest thy flock to rest at noon.' That question expresses an intense longing for Christ's manifest presence. Do we know anything about this? Is there in our souls an intense longing to be in the sweet fellowship of Christ?

It is both wise and comforting to God's people to flee to Christ in every time of need (Heb. 4:16). The ungodly rush to and fro in search of help and peace. They find no real consolation anywhere. But the believing heart flies as naturally to Christ as the rabbit to its den. In him alone can we find refuge for our souls.

Other refuge have I none,
Hangs my helpless soul on thee:
Leave, oh leave me not alone,
Still support and comfort me.

We have much that causes us to blush with shame before our beloved Saviour. We are black with sin. We labour too much for the cares of this world. We are terribly neglectful both of our Lord and our own souls. Still, though we are so full of evil, and so un-worthy of his grace, we must cling to Christ. He is all we have and all we want. Indeed, this is the very reason why we must cling to him!

We must never let our sins keep us from Christ. Under a sense of sin do not run from him but rather run to him. Sin may well drive us away from Moses and Mt Sinai, but it ought to draw us to Christ and Mt Calvary. Christ will not reject us because of our sin. He will not deal with us harshly when we run into his arms. Rather, he will comfort and protect all who do.

Notice the spirit in which this question is asked. It is not, 'O thou whom my soul believes in.' That would be true; but she has gone further. It is not, 'O thou whom my soul honours.' That is true, too; but she has passed beyond that stage. Nor is it merely, 'O thou whom my soul trusts and obeys.' She is doing that; but she uses warmer and more tender language than that. Her soul is full of fire and enthusiasm. She says, 'Tell me, O thou whom my soul loveth.'

This question arises from a heart of love for Christ. Whatever she may feel herself to be, she knows that she loves him. She is black and ashamed of herself, but still she loves her Bridegroom. She has not kept her own vineyard as she should have. She knows that and acknowledges it. Still, she loves him. She loves him as she loves no one else in all the world. Only Christ could claim such a title as this — 'Thou whom my soul loveth.' No one in all the world can be compared to him. He has no rival. He is the Lord of every believer's heart. He is the Monarch of our affections.

Our love, to be sure, is not worthy of him, but we love him supremely and we love him intensely. It is this love for Christ that governs our hearts and motivates our lives (2 Cor. 5:14). Others serve by the rigorous rule of the law. The believer serves Christ from a heart of love. Settle this matter in your own heart. Do you love the Lord Jesus Christ (1 Cor. 16:22)? Do you serve him out of fear? Do you serve him because of your desire for gain? Or, do you serve him because you love him?

This question is addressed to Christ himself. 'Tell me, O thou whom my soul loveth, where thou feedest, where thou makest thy flock to rest at noon.' She goes directly to him. She desires to have him speak directly to her heart. We love to hear the gospel. We love to read the gospel message. But the thing we desire is to hear it from Christ himself. If he will but speak the Word directly to our hearts by the power of his Spirit, then our souls shall be fed and refreshed.

Now, look at the question itself. She desires to know where Christ is and where he feeds his flock, where he meets with and refreshes his people. 'Tell me, O thou whom my soul loveth, where thou feedest, where thou makest thy flock to rest at noon.' What is the bread with which the Son of God feeds his people's souls? It is the gospel of God's free and sovereign grace in him — sovereign election, effectual redemption, free justification, absolute forgiveness, immutable grace, and everlasting love (Jeremiah 6:16). What are those promises by which the Lord Jesus comforts and refreshes his own in the heat of the day? They are sure covenant promises, which are 'yea and amen' in him.

2. An argument urged

Being in earnest about her soul and her Beloved, the bride is not content merely to raise a question. She presses for an answer, urging her question with an argument: 'For why should I be as one that turneth aside by the flocks of thy companions?'

John Gill suggested that these 'companions' are not real companions of Christ, 'But false friends, hypocrites and heretics, rivals with him, who set up schemes of worship and doctrine in opposition to his.' He was probably right. Satan is a wise and crafty enemy to our souls. He knows that we are not likely to turn aside and follow men who openly oppose Christ. Therefore, he makes his ministers the ministers of righteousness (self-righteousness). We are ever pressed to turn aside from Christ to pursue this or that.

There are many pretended companions of Christ, who allure our souls. There has always been an abundance of false teachers and those who follow them. Some have been turned aside from worship in the spirit to religious ritualism. Others have been turned aside from looking to Christ alone for righteousness to a legal righteousness of their own making. Some have turned aside from free grace to free will, from the gospel of Christ to Arminianism. Many are turned from Christ by pressure from husband or wife. There are many who turn aside from the gospel of Christ to provide religious entertainment for their children. Many are turned aside from the simplicity of Christ crucified to search out 'deeper' things: church order, prophetic mysteries, and Bible codes. Multitudes are turning aside to legalism. They leave Christ for Moses. They forsake Calvary for Sinai. They turn from grace to law.

Be warned! Satan does not care what you turn to, so long as you turn from Christ. If he can get you to leave Christ for anything, he has won the day. Why should we be as those who turn aside by the flocks of Christ's pretended companions, when we can walk with Christ himself? It grieves me to see any leave Christ, turning aside to follow something or someone other than Christ. But why should we be turned aside from him?

When the multitudes turned and walked no more with Christ, he turned to his disciples and said, 'Will ye also go away?' With Peter we must answer, why should we be turned aside unto the flocks of thy companions? 'Lord, to whom shall we go?' We have found all that we need and desire in him.

Why should we turn aside by the flocks of others and miss his fellowship? There may be reason for others to leave him, but not for us. His rich, free, eternal, redeeming love has bound us hand and foot, so that we cannot leave him.

If it should ever come to pass that the local church or denomination of which you are a member turns aside from Christ, you will be wise to turn aside from that church and denomination (Rev. 18:4); but do not turn aside from Christ. Why should we leave him (Lk. 22:35)? Is there anything your soul needs that you do not find in him in infinite abundance? Is not his pardon sufficient? Is his righteousness not enough? Is there another comforter to compare to his Spirit? Is anyone or anything more effectual to reprove our sin and unbelief, or to motivate our hearts?

Let us endeavour to live in fellowship with Christ himself. We seek not the blessings of his hand but the presence of his person. It is good to have the truth of Christ, but it is better to have Christ himself. If we miss his fellowship, if we turn aside from him, his truth will have no aroma. If we lose fellowship with Christ, we will have the standard, but not the Standard Bearer. We might have the candlestick, but there will be no light upon it. If we miss the fellowship of Christ, will we not be stripped of our strength, our joy, and our comfort?

Let us take up this prayer and make it our own: 'Tell me, O thou whom my soul loveth, where thou feedest, where thou makest thy flock to rest at noon: for why should I be as one that turneth aside by the flocks of thy companions?'

Thou, O Christ, art all I want!
More than all in thee I find!

3. An answer obtained

She asked him where he fed, where he made his flock to rest at noon. And now the Lord Jesus replies to his beloved bride. He speaks in love to comfort her heart and assure her. First, the Lord tells us how beautiful his people are in his eyes (vv. 8-11). In our own eyes, and in the eyes of others, we are black and scornful. But in his eyes we are fair and comely. I would rather trust his eyes than my eyes. If my eyes tell me that I am black, I will weep. But if he assures me that I am fair in his eyes, I will believe him and rejoice. This is what the Son of God says to all who are washed in his blood, robed in his righteousness, and united to him by faith. 'O thou fairest among women...I have compared thee, O my love, to a company of horses in Pharaoh's chariots. Thy cheeks are comely with rows of jewels, thy neck with chains of gold. We will make thee borders of gold with studs of silver.'
Christ sees us in the beauty of his own imputed righteousness and declares that we are perfectly beautiful (Ezek. 16:13-14).

In thy Surety thou art free.
His dear hands were pierced for thee:
With his spotless garments on,
We're as holy as God's own Son!

Christ does not exaggerate the beauty of his people. In him we are perfectly beautiful and gloriously complete, so much so that we may confidently exclaim, 'Who shall lay anything to the charge of God's elect?' This is not only what we shall be, experimentally, when he is finished with us (Eph. 5:25-27), this is what we are in him now!
In this passage (vv. 9-11), our Lord uses a well-known picture of royal beauty to typify the beauty of his people in him. He compares us to a company of horses in Pharaoh's chariots. Each one is specially chosen, very costly, exceedingly beautiful, and very strong. Next, he shows how he has adorned us by his grace, with rows of jewels, the graces of the Holy Spirit (Gal. 5:22), and chains

of gold, the blessings of graces in him (Eph. 1:3-14). Then he tells us what will yet be done for us: 'We' (God the Father, God the Son, and God the Holy Spirit), 'We will make thee borders of gold with studs of silver.' This is obviously symbolic, picturing our everlasting bliss and glory with Christ in the heavenly Jerusalem (Isa. 54:11-12; Rev. 21:18-21).

Now, look at the Lord's answer to our question. 'Tell me, O thou whom my soul loveth, where thou feedest, where thou makest thy flock to rest at noon: for why should I be as one that turneth aside by the flocks of thy companions? If thou know not, O thou fairest among women, go thy way forth by the footsteps of the flock, and feed thy kids beside the shepherds' tents' (vv.7-8).

Here is his word of instruction for our hearts: 'Go thy way forth by the footsteps of the flock, and feed thy kids beside the shepherds' tents.' He tells us where to find him, where to find food and rest and refreshment for our souls. If you would find Christ, you will find him in the way of the holy prophets, in the way of the patriarchs, and in the way of the apostles. Follow the footsteps of the flock, feed by the tents of his shepherds, and you may find him.

What are the footsteps of the flock? They are the paths in which God's people have always walked. They are the paths of the Lord's sheep. They are not hard to find. They are plain and clear. Abraham, Isaac, and Jacob walked in these paths. These are the paths of David, Isaiah, and Jeremiah. Peter, James, John, and Paul followed these paths. Let us walk in them, too. 'The footsteps of the flock' are the path of faith and trust, submission and obedience, righteousness and godliness, love and kindness, and doctrinal truth (Jer. 6:16).

Who are these shepherds, by whose tents we must feed? There are many in these days who have set themselves up as shepherds, who feed their sheep in poisonous pastures. Keep away from them. Do not follow a man. Do not cling to a church. Find a man who is preaching the gospel of Christ, and feed by his tent. The church where the gospel is preached is the shepherds' tent. The man who is preaching the gospel is one of Christ's shepherds (Jer. 3:15). Find a man who is like Paul, 'Determined not to know anything among you save Jesus Christ and him crucified', and you can safely feed by his tent. Those who are the true servants of Christ preach Christ, they preach all of Christ, and they preach nothing but Christ.

Let others turn aside if they must to the empty cisterns of religious philosophy. We have found a refreshing fountain of life in Christ himself, and we have found rich pastures for our souls in these blessed doctrines of the gospel.

4.

Christ's estimate of his people

Song of Solomon 1:8-11

'O thou fairest among women, …I have compared thee, O my love, to a company of horses in Pharaoh's chariots. Thy cheeks are comely with rows of jewels, thy neck with chains of gold. We will make thee borders of gold with studs of silver.'

As we become increasingly aware of our personal sinfulness and corruption, as we are humbled by the depravity of our hearts, nothing is more comforting, cheerful, and reassuring to God's saints in this world than the knowledge of the fact that in the eyes of Christ we stand perfect in the beauty of his righteousness, the beauty which he has put upon us.

Indeed, all the spiritual goodness, beauty, and comeliness we have before God is that which Christ puts upon us! We are washed in his blood, robed in his righteousness, and created in his image. How blessed it is, when most keenly and painfully aware of the fact that in us, in our flesh dwelleth no good thing, to hear our Saviour say, 'Thy beauty is perfect through my comeliness, which I put upon thee' (Ezek. 16:14).

In its essence, that is what the Song of Solomon is all about. This blessed book is a song of love between Christ and his church. As we read the book, we who belong to Christ, we who are married to the Son of God ought to make it as personal as possible.

Whenever the bride speaks, read it in the first person. Her words are the expressions of every believer's heart.

Whenever Solomon speaks to the bride, Pharaoh's daughter, read the words as the words of Christ speaking to you personally. All that he says to her shows the great love and high estimate Christ has for those who are chosen by him, washed in his blood and saved by his grace.

Throughout this blessed love song we see a constant fluctuation in the bride, but not in the Bridegroom. She varies greatly. Sometimes her heart burns with love for him. Then it is as cold as ice. Sometimes she delights to have him lie between her breasts. Then she bolts the door of her heart against him. But his love for her never changes! Is that not the way things are with you? Does your heart not ache and pine for a closer walk with Christ? Does not your heart cry out with Cowper…

> Oh for a closer walk with God,
> A calm and heavenly frame;
> A Light to shine upon the road
> That leads me to the Lamb.
>
> Where is the blessedness I knew
> When first I saw the Lord?
> Where is the soul-refreshing view
> Of Jesus in his Word?
>
> What peaceful hours I then enjoyed,
> How sweet their memory still!
> But now I find an aching void
> The world can never fill.
>
> Return, O holy Dove, return,
> Sweet Messenger of rest!
> I hate the sins that made thee mourn
> And drove thee from my breast.

The record of our constant need

The Song of Solomon is an inspired record of the constant languishings and revivings we experience in this world, the languishings of our hearts because of sin and the sweet revivings of our souls by our Saviour's unfailing grace.

'The song of songs, which is Solomon's' (v. 1).

What a proper, fitting, appropriate title that is for this book. Solomon means 'peaceful'. He represents Christ, the Prince of Peace, our beloved, all-glorious Saviour. This is not just a song. It is called 'The Song of Songs'. There are many songs recorded in the pages of Holy Scripture. Moses, Aaron and Miriam, Deborah, Hannah and David all sang songs, great and good songs unto the Lord. But this is called 'The Song of Songs'. All those other songs were songs of battles fought and victories won, trials endured and triumphs experienced. But this is purely a song of love. It is Solomon's song and it is all about Solomon. That is to say, it is Christ's song and it is all about Christ and his great love for us.

'Let him kiss me with the kisses of his mouth: for thy love is better than wine. Because of the savour of thy good ointments thy name is as ointment poured forth, therefore do the virgins love thee. Draw me, we will run after thee: the king hath brought me into his chambers: we will be glad and rejoice in thee, we will remember thy love more than wine: the upright love thee' (vv. 2-4).

These verses express the ardent desires of the believer's languishing heart for fresh discoveries of Christ's love and fresh, sweet, tokens of it from the kisses of his mouth.

'I am black, but comely, O ye daughters of Jerusalem, as the tents of Kedar, as the curtains of Solomon. Look not upon me, because I am black, because the sun hath looked upon me: my mother's children were angry with me; they made me the keeper of the vine-yards; but mine own vineyard have I not kept' (vv. 5-6).

Believers frankly and honestly confess their sin, the blackness of their hearts, their natures, and their lives. Yet, in the teeth of our sin, we look to Christ and claim the beauty that he has given us by grace. In our many trials and afflictions, we are often careless and fail to keep our own vineyards. Every heaven-born soul knows and freely confesses his sin (1 John 1:9).

'Tell me, O thou whom my soul loveth, where thou feedest, where thou makest thy flock to rest at noon: for why should I be as one that turneth aside by the flocks of thy companions?' (v. 7).

Here is an ardent expression of love for Christ, followed by an earnest prayer for guidance and grace. While we live in this world, we seek to follow Christ and feed at his table. But there are many false prophets and apostate churches, all claiming to be his companions. Therefore, we constantly look to our beloved Lord to direct our steps and keep us in the footsteps of his flock.

'If thou know not, O thou fairest among women, go thy way forth by the footsteps of the flock, and feed thy kids beside the shepherds' tents. I have compared thee, O my love, to a company of horses in Pharaoh's chariots. Thy cheeks are comely with rows of jewels, thy neck with chains of gold. We will make thee borders of gold with studs of silver' (vv. 8-11).

This is our Saviour's response to the confession of his beloved bride, telling us where he feeds his flock and makes them rest. This is what the Lord Jesus Christ thinks of his people.

A reminder of our ignorance

The bride asked her beloved where he feeds his flock, where he makes his flock to rest at noon. In our text he replies to his beloved bride, reminding her of her ignorance. The phrase, 'If thou know not', would be better translated, 'Since you do not know.' The question asked in verse 7 was an acknowledgment of ignorance. This reminder of the fact of our ignorance in all things spiritual is given not to discourage us, but to remind us that we must never cease looking to him for guidance and direction.

Particularly, he is reminding us that though we know something of our sinfulness, the corruption and deceitfulness of our hearts, we really have no idea just how corrupt and deceitful our hearts are. We know we are weak, but we do not really have any idea just how weak. We must ever look to him for strength to resist temptation, trust him, obey him, and walk in his way.

Instructions for where to find him

Here is his word of instruction for our hearts: 'Go thy way forth by the footsteps of the flock, and feed thy kids beside the shepherds' tents.' Here we are told where to find our Lord, where to find food and rest and refreshment for our souls. If we would find Christ, we will find him in the way of the holy prophets, in the way of the patriarchs, and in the way of the apostles. Only as we follow the footsteps of the flock and feed by the tents of his shepherds, will we find him.

'The footsteps of the flock' are the paths in which God's people have always walked. They are the paths of the Lord's sheep. They are not hard to find. They are plain and clear. Abraham, Isaac, and Jacob walked in these paths. These are the paths of David, Isaiah, and Jeremiah. Peter, James, John, and Paul followed these paths. Let us walk in them, too. They are the paths of faith and trust, of submission and obedience, of righteousness and godliness, of love and kindness, and the old paths of doctrinal truth (Jer. 6:16).

Who are these shepherds, by whose tents we must feed? There are many who set themselves up as shepherds, who would feed their followers in poisonous pastures of free will, works-religion. Keep away from them. Find a man who is preaching the gospel of God's free and sovereign grace in Christ, and feed by his tent. Only that church where the gospel is preached is the shepherds' tent. Only that man who is preaching the gospel is one of Christ's shepherds (Jer. 3:15).

Find a man who is like Paul, 'Determined not to know any-thing among you save Jesus Christ and him crucified', and you can safely feed by his tent. Those who are the true servants of Christ preach Christ, they preach all of Christ, and they preach nothing but Christ. The shepherds spoken of here are faithful gos-pel preachers, men appointed and called of God to be under shep-herds to Christ. The shepherd's tents are the churches pastored by God's faithful servants. As shepherds in ancient times pitched their tents in the wilderness where they led their flocks, so God's servants establish gospel churches in the wilderness of this world for the feeding of Christ's flock.

'Feed thy kids beside the shepherds tents.' We are here di-rected to feed our kids by the shepherds' tents, and nowhere else. The word 'kids' does not to refer to our physical children, though there is certainly an application to them. We are responsible to see to it that our children hear the Word of God faithfully preached. If you feed them upon the husks of free will, works-religion you will be responsible for their eternal ruin.

However, the word 'kids' is used here in reference to young converts, weak in faith and knowledge. They often think they know much and are strong; but that is not usually the case. Like young lambs, young believers are often a bit wild and rowdy, and have an offensive smell. But it is the 'kids' (lambs) of the flock who need our special care and patience.

Christ's estimate of his people

Here is Christ's estimate of his people. First, our Saviour tells us how beautiful his people are in his eyes: 'O thou fairest among women' (vv. 8-10). In our own eyes, and in the eyes of others, we are black and scornful. But in his eyes we are fair and comely. I would rather trust his eyes than my eyes. If my eyes tell me that I am black, I will weep. But if he assures me that I am fair in his eyes, I will believe him and rejoice.

This is our Redeemer's declaration to every believing sinner. 'I have compared thee, O my love, to a company of horses in Pharaoh's chariots. Thy cheeks are comely with rows of jewels, thy neck with chains of gold.'

The Son of God, our Mediator, sees us in the beauty of his own imputed righteousness and declares that we are perfectly beautiful. Yes, this is how we shall be when he gets done with us and presents us before the Father's throne (Eph. 5:25-27). But that is not what is spoken of here. Here our great God and Saviour is declaring what we are at this very moment in his eyes. This is no exaggeration, but a statement of fact (Ezek. 16:13-14). We are perfectly beautiful and gloriously complete, so much so that we may confidently exclaim, 'Who shall lay anything to the charge of God's elect?'

In thy Surety thou art free.
His dear hands were pierced for thee:
With his spotless garments on,
We're as holy as God's own Son!

In this passage (vv. 9-11), our Lord uses a well-known picture of royal beauty to typify the beauty of his people in him. He compares us to a company of horses in Pharaoh's chariots (beautiful, chosen, costly, strong). Then, he shows how he has adorned us by his grace, with rows of jewels (the graces of the Holy Spirit, Gal. 5:22) and chains of gold (the blessings of grace in him, Eph. 1:3-14).

In verse 11, our beloved Saviour tells us what will yet be done for us: 'We' (God the Father, God the Son, and God the Holy Spirit), 'We will make thee borders of gold with studs of silver.' This is a symbolic picture of the heavenly Jerusalem and our everlasting glory in heaven (Isa. 54:11-12; Rev. 21:18-21, cf. Eph. 5:25-27; Jude 24-25).

Let us never forget our personal weakness, ignorance, and sin. May God graciously cause us ever to look to Christ alone for strength, grace, and cleansing. Let us resolve, by God's grace, ever to be found walking in the footsteps of the flock, feeding by the shepherds' tents, as long as we are in this world. Let us always take special care to watch out and care for our younger brothers and sisters in the kingdom of God. Let us now remember what great things the Lord has done for us. Let us ever live in the anticipation of that glory which awaits us.

5.

Sitting with the King at his table

Song of Solomon 1:12-17

'While the king sitteth at his table, my spikenard sendeth forth the smell thereof. A bundle of myrrh is my wellbeloved unto me; he shall lie all night betwixt my breasts. My beloved is unto me as a cluster of camphire in the vineyards of Engedi. Behold, thou art fair, my love; behold, thou art fair; thou hast doves' eyes. Behold, thou art fair, my beloved, yea, pleasant: also our bed is green. The beams of our house are cedar, and our rafters of fir.'

Do you know this King? Is Jesus Christ your Lord, your Saviour, your King? Do you know the sweet taste of his saving grace? Have you experienced the blessedness of sins forgiven? Do you trust Christ? Are you washed in his blood, robed in his righteousness, and born of his Spirit? If you are, you are a sinner saved by the grace of God, saved through the blood of Christ, saved by the power of his Spirit. I am certain that your very soul longs, thirsts, pants, and hungers for him, like a love-sick young bride longs, thirsts, pants, and hungers for her husband. You want nothing like you want the embrace of his arms and the kisses of his mouth. That which we need and, I trust, desire above all things is communion with our all-glorious Christ.

The object of public worship

The object of public worship is that we may meet with and worship the Lord Jesus Christ, that we may sit with him at his table, have communion with him, and be fed by him. It is the presence of Christ that gives life and meaning to our worship. Our gatherings for worship without the fellowship of Christ are dreary business. It is like a brook without water, a cloud without rain, a sky without a sun, a night without a star. We need Christ! Without him all is vain! The doctrine of Christ without the presence of Christ is a lifeless corpse. The ordinances of Christ without the presence of Christ are meaningless rituals. Our songs of praise without the presence of Christ are but sorrowful groans. The Word of God without the presence of Christ is a sealed Book. The preaching of the gospel without the presence of Christ is only an exercise in futility.

We must have Christ, or we have nothing! We cannot live without him. Without him we have no light. Without him we have no comfort. Without him we have no strength. Without him we are nothing. Without him we can do nothing.

We have before us a picture of King Jesus sitting at his table, a table spread with the rich morsels of the gospel, manifesting himself to his people. We have here a picture of communion and fellowship with Christ himself.

Nothing so precious

There is nothing so precious to the true believer as Christ himself (vv. 12-14). Here, the bride speaks about her Beloved. 'While the king sitteth at his table, my spikenard sendeth forth the smell thereof. A bundle of myrrh is my wellbeloved unto me; he shall lie all night betwixt my breasts. My beloved is unto me as a cluster of camphire in the vineyards of Engedi.'

What a picture this is! The King is sitting at his table in his palace with his beloved bride. She is so overcome by his beauty and goodness that her heart must speak. In tender affection she tells him how precious he is to her. The picture, of course, is of our Lord Jesus Christ, sitting in the midst of his church in precious fellowship. Truly, our meetings are blessed when he meets with us. The gospel is truly a feast for our souls when he spreads the table. Christ is precious to believing hearts; and he is never more precious than at those times when he reveals and manifests himself in sweet, intimate, and real fellowship with his people (1 Pet. 2:7).

Here is the Lord Jesus Christ, the King (our King!), revealing himself in the blessedness of fellowship with his people (v. 12): 'While the king sitteth at his table, my spikenard sendeth forth the smell thereof.' This is the thing we most greatly desire at all times when we come together for worship. If Christ meets with us, all is well. It matters not where we meet, or even how many of us there are. If Christ is present, we have all that our hearts can desire.

All true believers reverence Christ as their sovereign King, bowing to him with willing, loving hearts. What bride would object to her loving and beloved husband being her king? Christ the King has his royal table spread in the gospel. The gospel of the grace of God is a feast of fat things prepared for all nations. It is a table furnished, by which the souls of men are fed. Our Lord has promised to be present with two or three who gather in his Name. He comes, by his Spirit through the ministry of his Word, to sup with us, and he allows us to sup with him.

When Christ himself meets with us, our meetings are truly blessed, because his presence draws out the grace he has created in our hearts. That is what is meant by the words, 'My spikenard sendeth forth the smell thereof.' As Mary broke open the box of precious spikenard and the sweet fragrance of it filled the room, so when the Lord Jesus meets with his people in the house of God, as the preacher breaks open the Word, the sweet fragrance of Christ crucified fills the room (John 12:1-3). When he withdraws and hides himself from us our spirits languish like tender plants in the hot sun. But when our Lord reveals himself our souls are renewed and made fruitful.

Nothing gives believing souls so much joy and satisfaction as fellowship with Christ. The children of God are not morbid people.

We know how to enjoy the good things of life. But the greatest joys known to men in this world are mixed with bitterness and sorrow. The blessed fellowship of Christ is pure joy. There are no bitter dregs in this sweet wine.

A bundle of myrrh

The Lord Jesus Christ is unutterably precious to every believer (vv. 13-14): 'A bundle of myrrh is my wellbeloved unto me; he shall lie all night betwixt my breasts. My beloved is unto me as a cluster of camphire in the vineyards of Engedi.'

Here we have a picture of our Lord's beauty, his value, and his love to a believing soul. The language is the language of intimate love. It is altogether spiritual. Christ is well beloved, the choice object of our hearts' affections. He is not merely beloved, but 'well-beloved'. He is chosen and preferred above all others. In our innermost souls his is uppermost. None can rival him. None can be compared with him.

The Lord Jesus is like a bundle of myrrh to us. Myrrh was a very costly and rare plant, greatly valued in ancient times for many reasons. It serves very well as a picture of Christ in this passage. Here are five ways in which myrrh fitly represents our Saviour:

First, Christ may be compared to myrrh because of its preciousness. It was a very expensive thing. It is always represented in Scripture as being rare and costly. Jacob sent some myrrh down into Egypt as a choice gift. But no myrrh could ever compare with our Lord Jesus Christ. He is the precious gift of God to us. When God gave us his Son, he gave us his all. What a precious gift Christ is to us! 'Thanks be unto God for his unspeakable gift!'

Second, Christ may be compared to myrrh because it was a very pleasant perfume. It was sweet to the smell. In the Old Testament, myrrh was mingled with the sacrifices so that when the fat of the kidneys of rams and beasts were burned the smoke that ascended up to heaven had the sweet fragrance of myrrh. Do you see the picture? That which makes us acceptable to God is the sweet perfume of our Lord Jesus Christ (1 Pet. 2:5). We are 'accepted in the beloved' (2 Cor. 2:15-16; Phil. 4:18; Mal. 1:11).

Third, Christ may be compared to myrrh because it was a preservative. The Egyptians used myrrh to embalm the dead. Nicodemus and those holy women who came to bury the Saviour brought myrrh and aloes to wrap his body. Myrrh was used to prevent decay and corruption. Even so, Christ, like a bundle of myrrh, preserves us.

Fourth, Christ may be compared to myrrh because it was used for purification. In ancient times people thought that myrrh had certain medicinal qualities. In times of pestilence and plague they would carry a little bag of myrrh around their necks, hanging between their breasts, to serve as a disinfectant. They were not correct in their ideas. But this is certain: The Lord Jesus Christ has infinitely great medicinal value for our souls. His Name is 'Jehovah-rophi'. He declares, 'I am the Lord that healeth thee.' He heals the hearts of chosen sinners of the deadly plague of sin. He makes every believer pure and perfect before God.

Fifth, Christ may be compared to myrrh because women in ancient times used it as a beautifier. Before Esther was presented to Ahasuerus she prepared herself with myrrh. Oriental women thought that myrrh would remove wrinkles and soften the skin. I have no knowledge about such things, but I do know that nothing makes a believer beautiful except Christ. He removes every spot and blemish and wrinkle from all his people (Eph. 5:25-27).

Women in ancient times would very carefully take precious, costly, rare sprigs of myrrh, tie them together, and hang them in a bag between their breasts for all of these reasons. And for all of these reasons, we will cling to Christ. His presence, his fellowship is like a bundle of myrrh between our breasts. When we have him all is well. Child of God, cling to Christ. Keep him near you. Bind him to your heart.

'He shall lie all night between my breasts.' This is an expression of intense desire. These are the words of confident faith. He said he would! This is a firm resolve. Throughout the long night of my pilgrimage through this world, I want his fellowship. If Christ will be with me, I want no more! 'He shall lie all night between my breasts.'

A cluster of camphire

Christ is our only acceptance before God (v. 14). 'My beloved is unto me as a cluster of camphire in the vineyards of Engedi.' The word translated 'camphire' is most commonly translated 'atonement', 'covering', or 'propitiation'. The Lord Jesus Christ is a cluster of merit and righteousness to all believers. He is precious to us, because he is our propitiation before God.

I do not suggest that Christ is so fully precious to all people. He is not. Multitudes see nothing in him. But no matter what he is or is not to another, *every* heaven-born soul speaks like this about Christ: 'My Beloved is unto me all that is needful, all that is lovely, all that is precious. He loved me and gave himself for me. He is my Lord and my God'; 'Unto you therefore which believe, he is precious!'

Nothing so precious to Christ

As there is nothing in all the world so precious to the believer as Christ, so nothing in all the world is so precious to the Lord Jesus Christ as his church (v. 15). Here the Lord Jesus speaks to us about us. 'Behold, thou art fair, my love; behold, thou art fair; thou hast doves' eyes.' So precious are the chosen to the Lord God that he will sacrifice nations for them (Isa. 43:4).

It is one thing for us to speak of Christ with great delight and satisfaction. But here is something that would be utterly unbelievable, were it not written in the Book of God. The Son of God, our all-glorious Christ, speaks of all who are united to him by faith, with delight and satisfaction! Yes, the Lord Jesus Christ has great delight in his church. Every true believer is beautiful in his eyes! 'Behold, thou art fair, my love; behold, thou art fair: thou hast dove's eyes.'

In his eyes we are perfectly beautiful! There is no cause for pride or for arrogance on our part. We have no beauty of our own. But his beauty is upon us, and he delights in that which he has made us to be in himself. The beauty Christ beholds in us is the real beauty of all true believers. Yet, the only beauty Christ looks upon with delight is the beauty he has created. We must never cease to be humbled by our own blackness, and never cease to rejoice in the beauty which Christ has given us. The Son of God looks upon us as we really are in him (1 Cor. 1:30; 6:11). And he looks upon us as we shall one day be (Eph. 5:27).

Our Lord also here assures us of his special, peculiar love for us: 'My love.' The Lord Jesus Christ holds his own elect near to his heart as the objects of his special love and favour. He speaks not to the world but to his own chosen and beloved companion, his bride, his church, when he says, 'My love.' The love of Christ for our souls truly is special. It is a sovereign, selective, sacrificial, saving, and satisfying love, and more. Christ's love for his own is an immutable, indestructible, everlasting love!

The one aspect of beauty, which our Lord mentions is that his people have the eyes of a dove. They have eyes that are enlightened and guided by the Dove of heaven, God the Holy Spirit. They have eyes that are loyal and faithful — eyes for Christ alone. They have weeping eyes that mourn as a dove (Ezek. 7:16).

Blessed pleasantness

When the Lord Jesus makes himself known to us and reveals his love to our hearts, all is pleasant (vv. 16-17). 'Behold, thou art fair, my beloved, yea, pleasant: also our bed is green. The beams of our house are cedar, and our rafters of fir.'

It is really impossible for me to say who is speaking here, Christ or the bride; but it really makes no difference. The message is the same whether coming from the bride or the Bridegroom. Yet, recognizing his beauty, and recognizing that whatever beauty we may have he has given us, we would turn all attention and praise to our beloved Lord. He is fair in himself. We are fair only in him.

Our marriage to Christ is a blessed, happy, fruitful union (Rom. 7:4). 'Our bed is green.' Our union with Christ is a firm and lasting union. 'The beams of our house are cedar.' It is both an ancient and durable union, a union that shall never be broken. And our fellowship with Christ is most delightful. 'Our rafters of fir.'

The word 'rafters' literally means 'galleries' or 'balconies', the porches that extend out from the bedroom, where the bride and groom sit and walk together in intimate fellowship. These galleries were made of fir, a fragrant and durable wood. Perhaps these galleries have reference to the Word of God and the ordinances of divine worship in the assembly of the saints. Perhaps they refer to our times of private prayer, worship, and meditation. Perhaps they refer to all the blessed doctrines of the gospel and all the blessings the grace of God revealed in it. The galleries, wherein we walk with our Saviour in sweet, intimate communion, include all these and more. They are all those things wherein the Son of God makes himself known to our hearts, all those things that cause our hearts to say with Peter, 'He is precious!'

6.

'I am sick of love'

Song of Solomon 2:1-7

'I am the rose of Sharon, and the lily of the valleys. As the lily among thorns, so is my love among the daughters. As the apple tree among the trees of the wood, so is my beloved among the sons. I sat down under his shadow with great delight, and his fruit was sweet to my taste.) He brought me to the banqueting house, and his banner over me was love. Stay me with flagons, comfort me with apples: for I am sick of love. His left hand is under my head, and his right hand doth embrace me. I charge you, O ye daughters of Jerusalem, by the roes, and by the hinds of the field, that ye stir not up, nor awake my love, till he please.'

Have you ever experienced love-sickness? Love-sickness is that sickness you get when someone dear and precious to you, someone you love is absent. It is that sick feeling you get when the one you love is absent from you and worse, there is a wedge between you. That is what is set before us in these verses. Only, the love-sickness before us here is altogether spiritual. It is a love-sickness between the believer's soul and Christ, our Well-Beloved, a sickness caused by our sin.

In this chapter we have another picture of that intimate love which exist between Christ and his church and the blessedness of our fellowship of love with our Redeemer. That which we most highly value and most greatly desire as the church of Christ is the constant fellowship of his manifest love.

> When I can say, 'My God is mine';
> When I can feel thy glories shine;
> I tread the world beneath my feet,
> And all the world calls good or great.

Assured security

We know and rejoice in the fact that Christ is the omnipresent God (Psa. 139:7-12). We know that Christ is always present with his people (Isa. 43:1-2; Matt. 28:20; Rev. 1:13, 16, 20). We know that Christ always meets with his people, as often as we gather in his Name (Matt. 18:20; 1 Cor. 3:16, 17). We know that Christ is always with each of his people (1 Cor. 6:19). We know that Christ always loves his people (John 13:1). We know that Christ always does what is best for his people (Eph. 1:22). And we know that Christ will ultimately bring all of his people to be with him in heaven. He will present us faultless, blameless, unreprovable, and perfect in heavenly glory (Eph. 5:25-27).

Without question, our souls are secure in Christ. All that concerns the eternal welfare of God's elect is safe. The Lord Jesus Christ will keep his church, which he purchased with his own blood, in perfect safety. Truly, at all times, it is well with my soul.

> When peace, like a river, attendeth my way,
> When sorrows, like sea billows roll,
> Whatever my lot, thou hast taught me to say,
> It is well, it is well with my soul.

All of these things are true. They are a source of comfort and joy to believing hearts at all times. Still, there are times when our Lord withdraws his manifest presence from us. There are times when we are unable to sense and perceive the reality of his presence with

us (S. of S. 5:6). This is the thing we greatly fear. We have no fear
of Christ ever leaving us entirely. That he will not do. But we do
fear losing the manifest presence of our beloved Lord. We do fear
losing the blessedness of his fellowship.

Sometimes he withdraws himself from us because of our sin,
our unbelief, or our neglect, as we shall see when we get to chapter
five. Sometimes he withdraws himself in order to increase in us
the awareness that we do truly need him. Whenever he is pleased
to withdraw his manifest presence from us, it is for our own good.
He intends to awaken us. He intends to draw out our hearts love
for him. He intends to return unto us. He promises, 'If I go away,
I will come again...I will not leave you comfortless.' Yet, for us it
is a sad, sad time when Christ withdraws the sweet manifestation
of himself. When he does, our worship is empty, our usefulness is
diminished, and our joy is gone. We are compelled to sing with
Newton, in low, bass tones...

How tedious and tasteless the hours,
When Jesus no longer I see;
Sweet prospects, sweet birds, and sweet flowers
Have all lost their sweetness to me.
The mid-summer sun shines but dim;
The fields strive in vain to look gay.

Then, our very hearts cry, 'I am sick of love.' There is a heavenly love-sickness in our souls for Christ. We want him. There are
five things in this passage that will help to show you what I mean
when I say this is one sickness I hope you will catch. 'I am sick of
love.'

A loving comparison

It is common with lovers to use poetic comparisons to describe one
another. And in the first three verses of this chapter both Christ and

his bride use poetic comparisons to describe their love and esteem for one another.

Christ, our Beloved Redeemer, speaks first (vv. 1-2). 'I am the rose of Sharon, and the lily of the valleys. As the lily among thorns, so is my love among the daughters.' He describes himself. Then, he describes those people whom he has loved, chosen, redeemed, and called unto himself. Our beloved Saviour is to all of his people, 'The Rose of Sharon' and 'The Lily of the valleys'.

'The Rose of Sharon'. This speaks of his redeeming blood. Though in the eyes of the world it is obnoxious, to us it is precious. The Rose of Sharon gives off the sweet smelling nectar of redeeming love, pardoning grace, and complete atonement.

'The Lily of the Valleys'. Through the righteousness of Christ, we have been made pure and white as a lily. The word translated 'lily' is from a root word that means 'whiteness'. The lily is in the shape of an umbrella, and Christ's righteousness, like an umbrella, covers us. In our many valleys, Christ is our Lily, both to cover and to cheer us.

Then the Lord Jesus tells us that we who are united to him by faith and love are 'as the lily among thorns'. By the mighty operation of free grace, the righteousness of Christ has been imputed to us in justification and imparted to us in sanctification, so that we bear a likeness to our Lord, even here upon this earth. The church of God in this world is 'a lily among thorns'. The cares of this world, unbelieving rebels, and our own vile lusts are thorns, things that contribute nothing but pain. Yet, among these thorns, God's people stand by his grace in Christ as lilies.

In verse three the bride speaks of her Beloved. Here is a tender comparison of Christ, our beloved Saviour, to a fruitful apple tree. He is the Tree of Life in the Paradise of God. 'As the apple tree among the trees of the wood, so is my beloved among the sons. I sat down under his shadow with great delight, and his fruit was sweet to my taste.'

Christ is a fruitful Tree. He declares, 'From me is thy fruit found' (Hos. 14:8). He is a shade Tree. 'I sat down under his shadow with great delight.' His fruit is sweet. Oh, how sweet and refreshing to us! The fruit of this tree is eternal life, free forgiveness, complete justification, all the fullness of grace here, and all the fullness of glory hereafter!

A loving remembrance

'He brought me to the banqueting house, and his banner over me was love' (v. 4). Here the bride lovingly remembers and gratefully acknowledges that she has all the blessings of the King's house only because of the King's grace. She remembers the first time she came to know his love to her. Can you not recall those first revelations of the Saviour's love to your heart? 'He brought me into the banqueting house.' 'His house of wines', or 'His place of feasting.'

Christ's banqueting house is the church of the living God. The table of feasting is spread with the truths of the gospel: covenant mercy, uncoditional election, substitutionary redemption, irresistible grace, final perseverance, everlasting glory. He took us by the hand and led us into his house. The wine of that house is the fellowship and communion of Christ himself. 'His banner over me was love' — Eternal love! — Special, distinguishing, electing love! — Redeeming love! — Persevering love! — Irresistible love!

A loving sickness

Remembering that which we have experienced and known of our Saviour and his grace, realizing that which is lost when our Lord withdraws himself, knowing something of the bliss and joy of his presence, when he hides his face our souls faint with a heavenly love-sickness. 'Stay me with flagons, comfort me with apples: for I am sick of love' (v. 5).

'I am sick of love!' More than anything in this world, we want him. We long for his presence. We want to know him. Our hearts cry, 'That I may know him, and the power of his resurrection, and the fellowship of his sufferings, being made conformable unto his death!' We want to know Christ in the fullness of his love. We want to know him in the fellowship of his suffering. We want to know him in the power of his resurrection (Eph. 3:19; Phil. 3:10). We long for his return. We long to be with him, and to know his manifest presence with us. So long as we remain in the body of flesh, so long as we must live here, among all the thorns of this sin-cursed earth, let us ever have the refreshing comfort of his grace.

'Stay me with flagons, comfort me with apples.' The flagons of wine represent the love of Christ. The apples represent the promises of the gospel. The promises of the gospel are as apples of gold in pictures of silver (Prov. 25:11).

A loving comforter

'His left hand is under my head, and his right hand doth embrace me' (v. 6). Our beloved Lord knows how to comfort our troubled and distressed hearts. John Gill wrote, 'The church, having desired to be stayed, supported, strengthened, and comforted, presently found her beloved with her, who with both hands sustained her.'

These words are expressive of many things. Surely, they speak of his tender love and care for us. They reflect the believer's intimate union and communion with Christ. And they display our safety and security in the arms of Christ. Is this now true? Has our beloved Lord and Redeemer come to us once again? Does he again hold and embrace us? If truly we are made to enjoy the fellowship of Christ, let us heed the admonition of verse seven.

A loving admonition

'I charge you, O ye daughters of Jerusalem, by the roes, and by the hinds of the field, that ye stir not up, nor awake my love, till he please.' Having experienced the sweetness of Christ's communion and the manifestation of his love, we greatly desire that they continue so long as we are upon the earth (Matt. 17:4). Yes, our Lord will come to us and withdraw himself from us according to his own wisdom and pleasure. We recognize those words, 'Till he please.' We bow to his will, even here. Yet, we must be careful that we do nothing to provoke him to leave us (Eph. 4:30). We must not neglect him and his love. We must take care not to grieve him (Eph. 4:23-32).

7.

'Winter is past'

Song of Solomon 2:8-15

'The voice of my beloved! behold, he cometh leaping upon the mountains, skipping upon the hills. My beloved is like a roe or a young hart: behold, he standeth behind our wall, he looketh forth at the windows, showing himself through the lattice. My beloved spake, and said unto me, Rise up, my love, my fair one, and come away. For, lo, the winter is past, the rain is over and gone; The flowers appear on the earth; the time of the singing of birds is come, and the voice of the turtle is heard in our land; The fig tree putteth forth her green figs, and the vines with the tender grape give a good smell. Arise, my love, my fair one, and come away. O my dove, that art in the clefts of the rock, in the secret places of the stairs, let me see thy countenance, let me hear thy voice; for sweet is thy voice, and thy countenance is comely. Take us the foxes, the little foxes, that spoil the vines: for our vines have tender grapes.'

Those things that are seen are types of the things that are not seen. The works of creation are pictures to the children of God that represent the secret mysteries of grace. God's truths are apples of gold; and the visible creatures are 'pictures' of silver (Prov. 25:11). In the verses before us, we have a picture of revival. It is a time of joy, refreshing, and singing. It is like springtime after a long, dreary winter. Here we see the Lord Jesus Christ coming to his church.

By his Word, by the manifestation of his presence, by his power, and by his grace, he brings a time of refreshing to his own beloved people.

I recognize that we are living in perilous times. We are living in the midst of the greatest religious apostasy ever known. It appears that the time has come when God has sent men a strong delusion that they should believe a lie because they received not the love of the truth. Freewill, works-religion is the greatest religious deception this world has ever known. This man-centred, man-exalting, man-pleasing, God-debasing, God-hating religion seems to engulf the entire world and all religious sects. The world, by-in-large, has accepted the doctrines of antichrist. These are indeed perilous times (2 Thess. 2:7-12; 2 Tim. 3:1-5; 4:3-4).

Any religion that is man-centred, any religion that has for its foundation man's will, man's works, or man's rights, any religion that promotes the honour, dignity, and pride of man, any religion that pampers and cultivates self-righteousness, self-esteem, and self-worth is antichrist.

Yet, it seems to me that, while we see apostasy all around us, God's church is also in the midst of revival. I see more men preaching the true gospel of God's free and sovereign grace than at any other time we know of in history. I am not talking about religious hirelings who discuss the doctrines of grace over coffee but dare not preach them in their pulpits. I am talking about men who boldly tell out God's truth. In the midst of wrath, our God does yet remember mercy. He has not forgotten to be gracious.

It appears to me that Christ is again working mightily in Zion. I hope that I am not deceived, but so far as the church of Christ, in its universal aspect, is concerned, I can almost hear the Saviour's voice crying, 'Rise up, my love, my fair one, and come away. For, lo, the winter is past, the rain is over and gone; The flowers appear on the earth; the time of singing birds is come, and the voice of the turtle dove is heard in our land.' I do not want to be presumptuous. Yet, I do not want to fail to recognize the hand of God's providence and his grace upon us.

In his wisdom and grace, the Lord sends upon his church some long, cold winters; but he also sends the springtime of revival to his beloved people. Anyone who reads the history of Christ's church, with half an eye open, will recognize that she has her ebbs and flows, her winter times and her spring times. Often it seemed as if she would be frozen out of the earth. Ungodliness, heresy, and error have prevailed at times. At other times she has been fruitful, triumphant, and majestic under the reviving influences of God the Holy Spirit.

Revival is not always a sudden burst of divine power upon the church. It is much more than a temporary emotional stirring. True revival is simply the communion and fellowship of Christ with his people. It often comes by degrees, by the gradual manifestation of Christ himself. Let's look at these verses and see what steps our Lord takes in coming to his people. In these verses of Inspiration, the Spirit of God shows us how it is that God brings revival to his church.

Christ comes

First, the Lord Jesus Christ comes to his people. 'The voice of my beloved! behold, he cometh leaping upon the mountains, skipping upon the hills. My beloved is like a roe or a young hart: behold, he standeth behind our wall, he looketh forth at the windows, show-ing himself through the lattice' (vv. 8-9).

It is our responsibility to seek the Lord and call upon him; but revival comes when he comes to us. The fact is, we will never truly seek him and call upon him, until he first seeks us and calls us. If he turns us, we shall be turned. If he calls us, we will run after him. Here we see the bride rejoicing in the approach of her Beloved (read Psalm 80).

She hears him speak. 'It is the voice of my beloved.' Christ calls to his church to tell us that he is coming. No one but Christ can speak to the heart; and no voice but his can make it burn. We are his sheep. We know his voice. He speaks to us through the preaching of the gospel. He speaks to us by his Spirit. He speaks to us personally. When he speaks, his bride, who knows his voice, says, 'It is the voice of my beloved!'

She sees him coming. 'Behold, he cometh.' The *eye* of faith looks for Christ, anticipating him. This may very well be taken as a prophecy of our Lord's first coming in the flesh. The incarnation of Christ to suffer and die as our Substitute was the hope and expectation of the Old Testament believers. Abraham rejoiced to see his day and was glad. The nearer the time came, the more clearly they saw. Those who waited for the consolation of Israel with an eye of faith saw him coming and rejoiced in God's salvation. They had heard him say, 'Lo, I come.' And faith responded, 'Behold, he cometh!' (Psa. 40:7-8). Blessed be his Name, the Lord Jesus came to redeem us!

He came cheerfully and with great speed, leaping and skipping over the mountains like a deer, as one who was pleased with the work before him. He was not a forced, but a voluntary Surety. Our Lord's heart was in the work of redemption (Isa. 50:5-7; Lk. 12:50).

The Son of God came to remove the difficulties that stood in the way of our salvation and to triumph over our enemies. He came 'leaping over the mountains'. The powers of darkness, our own sins, and the terrible curse of God's law had to be overcome. But before the determination of his love, these mountains were brought low.

He came suddenly and soon after the promise was given. God's people thought that the time between the promise and the fulfilment of the promise was very long. But it was not. One day the promise was given, and four days later the time came. At the appointed time Christ came. The due time was the best time (Rom. 5:6; Gal. 4:4-5).

This is true regarding our Lord's gracious visitations with his people today. His time is the best time. He withdraws himself, but for a small moment. At the appointed time, he will return to us in everlasting loving-kindness (Isa. 54:7-10).

This is also true regarding his glorious second advent. He says, 'Behold, I come quickly.' Faith responds, 'Behold, he cometh!' He has only been gone for two days! Soon, he shall appear in power and in great glory.

When the Lord Jesus comes to revive and refresh his people, he graciously reveals himself to our hearts. 'He standeth behind our wall, he looketh forth at the windows, showing himself through the lattice.' This was the condition of the church in the Old Testament. Christ was with them, but they did not clearly see him. He stood behind the wall of the law. He showed himself through the windows and lattices of their sacrifices and ceremonies. In a sense, this is the condition we are in as long as we are here upon the earth. Now we see him through a glass darkly. This body of flesh is a wall between him and us. But soon we shall see him face to face.

Particularly, these words describe our condition as believers when we are under a cloud. Christ is always near, but sometimes he is out of sight. He does not reveal himself to our hearts. The wall between us is a wall we have erected. The wall separating us from Christ is always 'our wall', our sins (Isa. 59:1-2). Our dear Saviour stands behind our wall as One who is waiting to be gracious, ready to be reconciled, willing to forgive (Rev. 3:20; See Hosea 14:1-4).

He graciously looks in at the windows and shows himself through the lattices to comfort us, to break us, and to make us open to him. The windows and lattices by which he shows himself are the ordinances he has given us. As we read his Word and seek his face in prayer, the Lord Jesus gives us glimpses of his face. As we hear the gospel preached in the house of God, sing his praise, and remember him in the Supper, eating the bread and drinking the wine, he shows himself. Each time a new born child confesses him in believer's baptism, symbolically buried in the watery grave and rising again in the newness of life, we see our Saviour in the glory of his redemptive accomplishments.

Christ calls

Second, once Christ has come to us and revealed himself, causing our hearts to burn for him, he lovingly calls us to himself. 'My beloved spake, and said unto me, Rise up, my love, my fair one, and come away. For, lo, the winter is past, the rain is over and gone; The flowers appear on the earth; the time of the singing of birds is come, and the voice of the turtle is heard in our land; The fig tree putteth forth her green figs, and the vines with the tender grape give a good smell. Arise, my love, my fair one, and come away' (vv. 10-13). Would to God we were all keenly sensitive to our Saviour's voice. Let us be like Abraham, Samuel, and Isaiah, ready to hear his voice, ready to obey him, ready to do his will.

In all of our frames and circumstances, Christ's love and attitude toward us is unchanged. His chastisements are the chastisements of a loving heart. He calls us his 'love' and his 'fair one'. Our Lord's love for us is immutable (Mal. 3:6; Heb. 13:8). It is in no way dependent upon us. 'My soul through many changes goes; his love no variation knows.' In his eyes, we are always fair and lovely, because he has made us so.

Christ calls for us to arise and come away with him (vv. 10, 13). 'Wherefore he saith, Awake thou that sleepest, and arise from the dead, and Christ shall give thee light' (Eph. 5:14). With tenderness and earnestness he urges us to come to him. Arise from your bed of slothful indifference. Come away from your carnal amusement and worldly care. Come to Me! We have come to him. Let us ever be coming to our Beloved (1 Pet. 2:4) for the mercy and grace we need. He bids us do so (Heb. 4:16)

Then the Lord presses our hearts to come to him (vv. 11-13). He says, 'The winter is past.' Our long, hard, bitter winters will not last forever. They will pass away. But spring would not be so pleasant if it did not follow winter. The winter is past for now; but it will come again. So we must make provision for it now. The time of fruitfulness and singing has come.

When Christ comes and makes himself known, his people rejoice, and sing, and bring forth fruit. 'The rain is over and gone;

The flowers appear on the earth; the time of the singing of birds is come, and the voice of the turtle is heard in our land; The fig tree putteth forth her green figs, and the vines with the tender grape give a good smell. Arise, my love, my fair one, and come away.' Someone said the serpents are driven away by the smell of grape-vines. I do not know whether or not that is true. But I do know that the old serpent is driven away when our True Vine puts forth his tender grapes. This picture might easily be applicable to many things:

- Our Lord's First Advent
- The dawning of the gospel age
- The conversion of sinners
- The revival of Christ's Church
- The great Resurrection Day

Christ communes

Christ first comes to us, then, he calls us to himself, and, thirdly, our all-glorious Christ communes with his believing people. 'O my dove, that art in the clefts of the rock, in the secret places of the stairs, let me see thy countenance, let me hear thy voice; for sweet is thy voice, and thy countenance is comely' (v. 14). In the most gentle and loving tones, Christ speaks to the hearts of his people. God always deals with his children graciously, in love and tender-ness. Look at the loving description he gives of those who put their trust in him.

The church of God is compared to a dove. The dove is inno-cent, beautiful, humble, faithful, and peaceful. That is what God makes his people to be by his grace. The Lord Jesus has taken away our guilt by his blood atonement, putting our sins away. The Lord God has put upon every redeemed sinner the very beauty of Christ's perfect righteousness. He conquers the heart in conver-sion, humbling his chosen vessels of mercy in repentance and faith. He has betrothed his bride to him in faithfulness. And the Prince of

Peace makes his people a peaceable people. Christ's chosen bride (the church) is his dove. He owns her and delights in her. She can find no rest except in him. Sooner or later she must return to him, even as Noah's dove returned to the ark.

The church of God is a dove, hidden in the clefts of the rock, Christ Jesus. The believing soul may not always be sensible of Christ's presence. But he is always sensible of his souls need; and he takes refuge in the wounds of that One who was smitten in our stead. 'Rock of Ages, cleft for me, Let me hide myself in thee!'

As he is the Rock in which we hide, our Saviour is the stairs, or ladder, by which believing sinners ascend up to God and have access to and communion with him. The 'secret places' may, as John Gill suggested, 'have respect to the justifying righteousness of Christ, and atonement by him, hidden to other men, but revealed to them; and whither in distress they betake themselves, and are sheltered from sin, law, hell, and death, and dwell in safety.'

Sensing his own need for Christ, every believer finds a closet in the secret places of the stairs to seek the Lord. Our love for and communications of love to Christ are not things about which we make a public spectacle. Public passion is cheap, demeaning, and disgusting. Believers, those who love Christ, pour out their hearts' passions to him in the secret places of the stairs.

As his church and bride, we are the objects of Christ's peculiar love and tender care. All that our Lord does for us, or to us, or allows to be done, he does because he loves us. In his eyes, we are lovely. He delights in us. He wants to see our faces turned toward him. He wants to hear our voices calling upon him. He wants to commune with us and us with him. Oh, great wonder of grace! The Son of God delights to have such worthless worms as we are! He truly loves us!

Has Christ come to you? Have you heard his voice? Have you seen the Lord, showing himself through the windows and lattices of your own soul? Has he driven away your long winter and made your soul to sing, rejoicing in his love?

Christ admonishes

Fourth, our Lord Jesus Christ gives us a loving admonition. 'Take us the foxes, the little foxes, that spoil the vines: for our vines have tender grapes' (v. 15). The admonition he gives us is to guard against and suppress those little foxes, which destroy the tender vines and would disturb the peace of his beloved dove. This is a charge to every believer to suppress his own sinful nature. Those evils of our nature, that may seem little in our own eyes (anger, wrath, gossip, slander, peevishness, evil speaking), must be avoided for the good of Christ's kingdom. There are other 'little foxes' that would destroy the peace of God's church. They, too, must be taken out of the way. All doctrinal error, all that is contrary to the gospel of God's free and sovereign grace in Christ, every little fox of freewill, works-religion must be kept out of God's vineyard. Every little fox of schism, strife, and division must also be put away, lest they spoil the vine. For the honour of our Beloved, for the good of our own souls, and for the good of our brethren, we must constantly guard against these little foxes of hell.

8.

'My Beloved is mine and I am his'

Song of Solomon 2:16-17

*'My beloved is mine, and I am his: he feedeth among the lilies.
Until the day break, and the shadows flee away, turn, my beloved,
and be thou like a roe or a young hart upon the mountains of
Bether.'*

Someone said of verse 16, 'This is the happiest verse in the Bible.'
I think I might have to agree. 'My beloved is mine and I am his: he
feedeth among the lilies.'

Those words reflect a heart full of peace, assurance, contentment, and joy. But the very next verse casts a shadow over the
scene. There is a cloud in the sky. 'Until the day break, and the
shadows flee away, turn, my beloved, and be thou like a roe, or a
young hart upon the mountains of Bether.'

These two verses together reflect a state of mind with which
many of God's saints in this world are very familiar. They are believers. They do not doubt their saving interest in Christ. They are
confident that God has saved them by his almighty, free grace.
They know that Christ is theirs. Still, they do not always enjoy the
light of his countenance.

Do these words describe your condition? You know that he is
yours; but your soul does not always feed upon that blessed fact.
You are, in your heart, assured that you have a vital saving interest

in Christ; but you do not sense that his left hand is under your head and that his right hand embraces you. There are times when the believer sings tenor and bass at the same time. We sing with great delight...

> Blessed assurance, Jesus is mine,
> Oh what a foretaste of glory Divine!
> Heir of salvation, purchased of God,
> Born of his Spirit, washed in his blood.

At the same time we sing with Newton...

> How tedious and tasteless the hours
> When Jesus no longer I see;
> Sweet prospects, sweet birds, and sweet flowers
> Have all lost their sweetness to me.

It may be that there are some saints who are always at their best, who never lose the light of the Saviour's face, and whose communion with him is never disturbed. I am not sure that such people exist, though I acknowledge the possibility. But those believers with whom I am most intimate have a different experience. And those people I know who always boast of their constant bliss are not the most reliable people I know.

For myself, my own heart's experience is this. I have always had a mixture of joy and sorrow. Every year of my life has had a winter as well as a summer. Every day has its night. I have seen the clear shining of the Sun of Righteousness. And I have felt the heavy rains, the bite of frost, and the freeze of winter sleet in my soul. I have walked in the warm breezes of a summer's evening. And I have made my way through the snowy blizzards of winter's night.

Believers are like the oak tree. The sap is always present but it is not always flowing freely. We do, at times, lose our leaves. We have our downs as well as our ups. We have our valleys as well as our mountaintops. We are not always rejoicing. Sometimes we are

in heaviness through our manifold temptations. We are grieved by
the fact that our fellowship with Christ is not always full of raptur-
ous delight. At times, we have to seek him, crying, 'Oh, that I knew
where I might find him!'

This appears to me to be the sense of these two verses. They
are a song of both joy and sorrow. It is the sweet song of assurance;
but it is mingled with an earnest longing for fellowship. Though we
may experience times of spiritual trial, when our fellowship and
communion with Christ is broken, the assurance of our hearts that
we are accepted in the Beloved need not be broken.

Assurance is based upon Christ's finished work for us. Fellowship and communion with Christ vary with our daily experiences.
I do not always enjoy the company of my wife, because we are at
times separated by many miles; but I always enjoy the assurance
of her love. And I do not always enjoy sweet fellowship with Christ;
but I do enjoy this blessed assurance, 'My beloved is mine; and I
am his.'

Assurance

I want every child of God to know that it is possible for us to enjoy
the assurance of our personal interest in Christ. I do not suggest
that every believer has this assurance. But I do say that every believer should and can have an assurance of his personal, saving interest in Christ. These are the words of confident faith and blessed
assurance, 'My beloved is mine, and I am his.'

Most people look in the wrong places when they seek assurance. They try to find assurance in their experiences; but no experience will give assurance. Believers are honest. We know that our
most spiritual experiences are shot full of pride and sin. Many seek
assurance based upon their devotion to Christ; but no amount of
devotion will give assurance. Believers know that their devotion to
Christ is unmentionable, because our best devotion is horribly un-
true. Others, following the counsel they have been given, seek assurance based upon their personal righteousness; but no amount

of personal righteousness will give assurance. Believers recognize that all their righteousness is as filthy rags.

If we want assurance, we must stop looking at ourselves and look away to Christ. Look not to your experience, but to his expiation. Look not to your repentance, but to his ransom. Look not to your faith, but to his faithfulness. Look not to your works, but to his worth. Look not to your feelings, but to his fulness. Look not to your prayers, but to his promises. Look not to your righteousness, but to his righteousness!

Look to Christ alone. And look to Christ for everything! 'As ye have therefore received Christ Jesus the Lord, so walk ye in him' (Col. 2:6). How did you first come to Christ? Did you bring anything with you? No. You came as an empty handed beggar, a naked, wretched sinner, looking to him alone for all your righteousness, all your acceptance with God, all your atonement for sin, all your hope of life. Do not ever hope to rise above that level. To walk in the Spirit is to walk by faith in Christ, looking to him for everything. All who so trust Christ may with confident assurance and joy declare, 'My beloved is mine, and I am his.'

'My beloved' — Do you not delight to call Christ your Beloved? Certainly, he should be beloved by you. Who has done so much for you as Christ? Who has lavished you with such gifts? Who has shown you such love? If you do not love him, you are a lost soul, yet under the wrath of God (1 Cor. 16:22). All who are redeemed by his precious blood and saved by his matchless grace love him (1 John 4:19).

If you know him, you love him. I would not have you to be presumptuous. But I would have all of you who know Christ to call him 'My beloved.' He deserves this title in your heart. He redeemed you with his own precious blood. He adopted you into his family. He saved you by his matchless grace. He loved you with an everlasting love.

There was a time when he became the Beloved One of your heart. In 'the time of love' he revealed his love to you and created love in you for him. We are bashful about this and prefer never to speak to others of our love for Christ. When we hear others sing, 'Oh, how I love Jesus', our hearts cry, 'Oh, how I wish I could love him as I should!' Still, in the teeth of all our sin, in the teeth of all we know we are, we confess with Peter, 'Lord, thou knowest all things. Thou knowest that I love thee.' 'We love him because he first loved us.' His love for us preceded our love for him eternally. His love for us exceeds our love for him infinitely. And his love for us is the cause of our love for him. But we do love him. Not as we want! Not as we ought! Not as we shall! But every believer honestly confesses, 'We love him because he first loved us.' How our hearts rejoice to look upon the Son of God and say, 'My beloved is mine!' C. H. Spurgeon wrote, 'Every heart that has been renewed by sovereign grace takes Jesus Christ to be the chief object of its love.'

'My beloved is mine, and I am his!' — We are his by the bands of his eternal love. We are his by the grace of his sovereign, eternal election. We are his by the blood of his special purchase. We are his by the power of his almighty, irresistible grace. We are his by our own wilful, deliberate choice. Are you a believer? If so, then Christ is yours and you are his. You are the sheep of his pasture. You are the object of his love. You are the member of his body. You are the branch of his root. You belong to him. You are Christ's, totally, unreservedly his. You belong to him. You are not your own. He bought you with his blood.

Perhaps you think, 'I would do anything to have such assurance.' Would you do nothing? The basis of assurance is not what you do, but what Christ has done for you. The Holy Spirit requires that we 'be ready always to give an answer to every man that asketh you a reason of the hope that is in us with meekness and fear' (1 Pet. 3:15). What is the basis of this assurance? How can a person be assured that he has a saving interest in Christ? How can I know I am my Beloved's and that he is mine? I trust him. That's all. The whole of my assurance is faith in Christ. It is written, 'He that believeth on the Son of God hath everlasting life!'

His place

All who know Christ know where he is, where he reveals himself and makes himself known. The soul, being assured of its personal interest in Christ, longs to be where he is. 'He feedeth among the lilies.' The lilies are his people (v. 2). In this world they are lilies among thorns. Still the Lord Jesus feeds among them. The lily patch in which the Son of God feeds is the assembly of his saints (the house and temple of God) for public worship (Matt. 18:20; 1 Cor. 3:16-17). Here he feeds his people upon his grace by the Word of his grace.

The church of God has many critics, but no rivals. This is the family of God, the kingdom of heaven, the temple of the Holy One, the place where Christ manifests forth his glory, spreads his table, and meets with his people. Blessed beyond description are those people who are privileged to be a part of this family! Truly, as Paul puts it, this is 'a habitation of God through the Spirit'!

Our desire

It is the desire of every believer to know the conscious presence and fellowship of Christ. This is what is expressed in verse seventeen: 'Until the day break, and the shadows flee away, turn, my beloved, and be thou like a roe or a young hart upon the mountains of Bether.'

This is our night time. Soon our day will break. On that great day, all the shadows of darkness and ignorance will be forever gone! When the gospel day broke forth the shadows of the law fled away. The mountains that separate us from our Lord, he can overcome. They are too high for us, but not for him. Our hearts earnestly desire the conscious awareness of his presence, ever crying, 'Turn, my beloved' (See Psalm 42:1 and 84:2).

9.

'I will seek him'

Song of Solomon 3:1-5

'By night on my bed I sought him whom my soul loveth: I sought him, but I found him not. I will rise now, and go about the city in the streets, and in the broad ways I will seek him whom my soul loveth: I sought him, but I found him not. The watchmen that go about the city found me: to whom I said, Saw ye him whom my soul loveth? It was but a little that I passed from them, but I found him whom my soul loveth: I held him, and would not let him go, until I had brought him into my mother's house, and into the chamber of her that conceived me. I charge you, O ye daughters of Jerusalem, by the roes, and by the hinds of the field, that ye stir not up, nor awake my love, till he please.'

Those who love the Lord Jesus Christ seek his manifest presence. Nothing in all the world is more pleasant to the believing heart than communion with our Lord Jesus Christ. Those who enjoy the spiritual presence and fellowship of Christ are supremely favoured of God.

Holy Scripture exhausts every earthly figure to express the charms and delights of this blessed fellowship between Christ and his redeemed ones. It is impossible for human language to express the sweetness of his grace, the joy of his communion, and the comfort of his presence.

Just as it is the sweetest thing in the world to enjoy communion with Christ, it is the saddest thing in the world to a believer to be without the Lord's manifest presence and fellowship. Yet, that is just the condition that we see the church in at the beginning of this chapter: 'By night on my bed I sought him whom my soul loveth: I sought him, but I found him not.' But she was resolved not to rest in such a sad condition. She said, 'I will seek him.' She would not rest until she had found him and brought him into her mother's house. There she held him and would not let him go.

Spiritual presence

The Lord Jesus Christ is no longer physically present with his church. 'He is not here, for he is risen.' Our Lord's physical body is in heaven. There he sits upon the throne of God, making intercession for us according to the will of God and anticipating the day when his enemies shall be made his footstool.

The papists tell us that our Lord is bodily present with us in the mass. But that cannot be. 'Such persons unwittingly deny the real humanity of our Lord Jesus Christ, for if he has indeed assumed our humanity, and is in all points made like unto his brethren, his flesh and blood cannot be in two places at one time' (C. H. Spurgeon). Since our Lord, as a real man, the God-man, is in heaven, his bodily presence is no longer with his church.

We know that it is best for us that Christ is no longer present with his church in a physical sense, because he said so (John 16:7). As God, Christ is everywhere. He is omnipresent. As man, he is in heaven. His bodily presence is as much limited today to one place as it was when he was upon the earth. But as the God-man in one Person, the Mediator and Head of the church, Christ is present with us by the Holy Spirit, the Divine Comforter, whom the Father has sent in his Name.

It is by the working of God the Holy Spirit that Christ's presence with his church is manifested. We need not expect or desire anything other than this spiritual presence of Christ. By his Spirit,

Christ is everywhere present with his church at all times to guide, to protect, to instruct, and to comfort his people.

This spiritual presence of Christ is the glory of the church of God; and this is the thing we desire. When Christ is manifestly presence with us in this spiritual sense we have all that we need or desire. When this spiritual presence is absent, our strength and glory is gone.

I am afraid that the name of the church of the twentieth and twenty-first centuries might well be called 'Ichabod, The glory is departed from Israel!' If a church is without the Spirit of God, she may have a name to live, but it is dead; and, you know, that corruption follows death. Those churches that have turned aside unto error, have not only lost all power to do good, but they have become obnoxious, loathsome, and the causes of great evil in the world.

The one thing that we need is the spiritual presence of Christ. He said, 'Without me ye can do nothing.' But if Christ shall come to us in the Person of his blessed Spirit our power and our glory shall be restored. The return of the Lord's manifest presence by the Holy Spirit has been the birth of every true revival and spiritual awakening. The manifest presence of Christ in the midst of his people is the Sun of Righteousness arising with healing beneath his wings.

Seeking the Lord

We ought to constantly seek the Lord's manifest presence, both individually and for his church. Without question, wherever men and women gather in his Name to worship him, the Lord Jesus is present (Matt. 18:20). That gathered band of believers, if only two or three in number, is the temple of God (1 Cor. 3:16-17), 'an habitation of God through the Spirit' (Eph. 2:22), and 'the house of God—the church of the living God' (1 Tim. 3:15). I am thankful to say, it appears that our God is working among his people all over the country and around the world in our day. But if we are to see better and greater things in the days that lie ahead, we must ever seek the presence of Christ by the Holy Spirit. 'Not by might, nor by power, but by my Spirit, saith the Lord.' I urge you, my brother, my sister in Christ, to make this determined resolution. Fix it in your heart, and do not be turned aside from it —'I will seek him!' 'I will seek him whom my soul loveth.' You have been chosen of God in eternal election, redeemed by the blood of Christ, and called to life and faith in Christ by God the Holy Spirit.

If you are yet without Christ, without God, without hope, without life, I would press you into the kingdom. I urge you, for your soul's sake, to seek our Lord with all your heart. Seek him in his Word. Seek him by faith. Seek him now. If you seek him, you will find him. He has promised that he will be found by all who seek him. 'For I know the thoughts that I think toward you, saith the LORD, thoughts of peace, and not of evil, to give you an expected end. Then shall ye call upon me, and ye shall go and pray unto me, and I will hearken unto you. And ye shall seek me, and find me, when ye shall search for me with all your heart. And I will be found of you, saith the LORD: and I will turn away your captivity, and I will gather you from all the nations, and from all the places whither I have driven you, saith the LORD; and I will bring you again into the place whence I caused you to be carried away captive' (Jer. 29:11-14).

Those who seek

Here are seven things revealed in the Book of God about those who seek the Lord.

Those who seek Christ love Christ

In these five verses, the lovesick spouse speaks of Christ as 'him whom my soul loveth'. It may be that you do not now enjoy the manifestation of the Lord's presence; but your heart clings to him.

You may have been idle, slothful, neglectful, and sinful. You may have much to regret and much to weep over. But Christ is truly the One whom your soul loves. A loving wife may not always have her husband in her arms; but she always has him in her heart. Even so, the true believer does not always enjoy the presence of Christ, but he never ceases to love Christ.

The words are very strong: 'him whom my soul loveth.' It is as though she said, 'Though there are many whom I love, he is the love of my soul. My deepest, fondest, purest, truest, most real love is reserved for him alone. Do you have such a heart for Christ? Is he the Love of your soul? Is he the Object of your heart's affection? All true believers do sincerely love the Lord Jesus Christ. It is not possible for a person truly to know Christ and not love him. 'We love him because he first loved us' (1 John 4:19). Christ's love for us precedes our love for him. His love for us causes our love for him. His love for us infinitely exceeds our love for him. But we do love him.

We love the Lord Jesus Christ himself, because of who he is. This One whom we love is himself the eternal God; and he is perfect man. He is the God-man our Mediator. We love him because he has revealed himself in our hearts. We love Christ because of all that he has done for us. His love for us is manifest by his deeds. His love is not dormant and idle. All that he has done and is doing and shall do is motivated by his love for us.

Because he loved us, the Son of God assumed all responsibility for our souls as our covenant Surety before the world began (Heb. 7:22; Eph. 1:3-6; 2 Tim. 1:9). In the fullness of time, he assumed human flesh and came into the world in our nature to redeem and save us by his obedience to God as our Mediator, Representative, and Substitute (Matt. 1:21). Because he loved us, the Lord Jesus lived in perfect obedience to God's holy law to bring in everlasting righteousness as our Representative (Rom. 5:18-21). Because of his great love for us, the Darling of Heaven laid down his life as our Substitute that we might live forever through him (Rom. 5:6-11). Our risen Saviour rules the universe in love for his people, as the

God-man our Mediator King, to give eternal life to the objects of his everlasting love (John 17:2).

It is Christ himself that we love. Immanuel has won our hearts. We love him. Many love his doctrine; but we love him. Many love his throne; but we love him. Many love his church; but we love him. Many love his works; but we love him.

Those who seek Christ know their need of him

The spouse sensed that her beloved Bridegroom was gone; and she seems to be in desperate need of him. Do you know your need of Christ? If a person knows his need of Christ, he will seek him (Phil. 3:7-11). We need his righteousness to cover our shameful nakedness. We need his blood to cleanse us from our sins. We need his grace to save us and keep us. We need his wisdom to direct us. We need his strength to uphold and protect us. We need him! Our Lord told us plainly, 'Without me, ye can do nothing.' And we have found, by painful and blessed experience, that it is true. Without him, we cannot sing his praise. Without him, we cannot pray with understanding. Without him, we cannot worship in the Spirit. Without him, we cannot live in peace. Without him, we cannot know, do, or enjoy God's will. Without him, we cannot understand God's Word.

Those who seek Christ seek him diligently

Those who ardently love Christ and know their need of him do not cease to seek him, and seek him diligently. In this chapter we see the spouse seeking him upon her bed, seeking him in the streets, seeking him in the broadways, and finally seeking him at the lips of the watchman. She sought him in every place where he was likely to be found she left no stone unturned.

If you are truly in earnest in knowing Christ, if you are really concerned for your soul, if you truly thirst and pant for fellowship with the Son of God, you will diligently seek him. You will seek him in the closet of your heart in earnest prayer. You will seek him in the field of Holy Scripture. You will seek him in the assembly of his saints, in his house where he is most likely to be found. You will seek him through the preaching of the gospel, the means by which he reveals himself to sinners. Those men who preach the gospel of God's free and sovereign grace in Christ are the watchmen of Zion (Isa. 62:6; Ezek. 33:7; Heb. 13:7, 17). They are the watchmen to whom the spouse went, seeking her Beloved (S. of S. 3:3; 5:7). Public worship and gospel preaching are not optional things in spiritual life. They are vital to it. God has given his church pastors and teachers specifically for the purpose of watching over, instructing, and teaching his people (Eph. 4:11-16).

Those who diligently seek Christ will find him

Neither the brethren, nor the church of God, nor those who preach the gospel can comfort the afflicted conscience, unless Christ himself is apprehended by faith. But as soon as she left the watchmen she found him whom she sought. 'It was but a little that I passed from them, but I found him whom my soul loveth: I held him, and would not let him go, until I had brought him into my mother's house, and into the chamber of her that conceived me' (v. 4).

If the Lord Jesus hides himself from his people for a season, he has a reason. If we are stirred to seek him, it is Christ himself who has created in our hearts a need and desire for him. And, where the Lord Jesus Christ has created a desire for himself, he will give satisfaction. He comes to all who seek him. Matthew Henry wrote, 'Those that continue seeking the Lord shall find him at last, when perhaps they are almost ready to despair of finding him' (See Psa. 34:1-6; Isa. 54:7-10; Jer. 29:12-14).

Those who seek Christ, when they have found him, will hold him fast

They will take care to retain him. They will endeavour to maintain their fellowship and communion with him. Look at verse four again. 'I held him and would not let him go.' Yes, he will go away if we do not hold him; but he is willing to be held by us. More, he is the One who causes us to want to hold him and gives us grace to hold him. In other words, we hold him by faith (faith that he gives and maintains), because he holds us by grace. We hold him in the arms of love, because he holds us in the arms of his love. We hold him by earnest prayer, because he holds us by constant intercession. We hold him by willing submission and obedience, because he makes us willing, submissive servants.

Those who seek Christ, when they have found him, will bring him into the house of God

When believers walk in fellowship with Christ, they bring him with them into the fellowship of the saints. Read verse four once more. 'It was but a little that I passed from them, but I found him whom my soul loveth: I held him, and would not let him go, until I had brought him into my mother's house, and into the chamber of her that conceived me.' Blessed are those local churches into which men and women bring the Son of God as they come together!

Those who seek Christ, when they have found him, will jealously guard his blessed presence

Our Lord is not indifferent about the conduct of his people. There are many things that will drive him from us and destroy our fellowship with him (Eph. 4:30). Anger, wrath and malice, pride, slander and vengeance, love of the world, envy and strife are all things that grieve the Holy Spirit of God, by whom we are sealed unto the day of redemption. Let us take care not to grieve him. Rather, let us walk in the Spirit, as followers of Christ, loving, forgiving, submitting to, and serving one another for the glory of God.

10.

Christic and his church in their royal chariot

Song of Solomon 3:6-11

'Who is this that cometh out of the wilderness like pillars of smoke, perfumed with myrrh and frankincense, with all powders of the merchant? Behold his bed, which is Solomon's; threescore valiant men are about it, of the valiant of Israel. They all hold swords, being expert in war: every man hath his sword upon his thigh because of fear in the night. King Solomon made himself a chariot of the wood of Lebanon. He made the pillars thereof of silver, the bottom thereof of gold, the covering of it of purple, the midst thereof being paved with love, for the daughters of Jerusalem. Go forth, O ye daughters of Zion, and behold king Solomon with the crown wherewith his mother crowned him in the day of his espousals, and in the day of the gladness of his heart.'

Try to picture the scene before us in this passage. A royal wedding has taken place. King Solomon has taken Pharaoh's daughter to be his wife. She is arrayed in all the beauty and splendour of a royal bride. Solomon, with all his wealth, has spared no expense for this glorious occasion. The wedding ceremony is now over. The marriage supper is ended. The royal pair, the newly wed king and his queen prepare to leave for their honeymoon. The king nods his head and his nuptial chariot is brought forward. It is a chariot he has especially prepared for his beloved bride. The magnificent coach will carry the happy couple through the wilderness to the place where their marriage will be consummated.

Standing in the front of the chariot are two men carrying torches to light their way through the wilderness. The torches burn with all the powders of the merchants, giving off in their smoke the fragrances of romantic perfume. In front of the chariot, on both sides, and in the rear there are sixty valiant men, selected by Solomon himself, to guard the royal pair as they make their way through the wilderness. Every man is expert in war and ready to die, if need be, in defence of the king and his bride. The chariot is made of the fine woods of Lebanon. Its four posts are of silver. The bottom of it is covered with gold. Its curtains are made of fine purple. Secluded behind those curtains, safe and happy, are the king and his bride upon their bed, a bed made by his own hands. They recline together upon the soft cushions of love he has prepared.

An allegory

The picture, of course, is an allegory referring to Christ and his bride, the church, whom he purchased with his own blood and conquered by his irresistible love. It pictures both the happiness and safety of the church of Christ as she is carried through the darkness and wilderness of this world in the arms of Christ. Resting in his love, secure in his arms, we can almost hear her speak: 'I will fear no evil: for thou art with me...Surely goodness and mercy shall follow me all the days of my life: and I will dwell in the house of the Lord forever.'

As this passage opens, the daughters of Jerusalem speak with astonishment. They are overcome with awe by the beauty and majesty that has been given to the church of Christ. It is not at all uncommon for new converts to be astonished by that which Christ has made his church to be. She who was once black and despised is now adorned with beauty and admired. Looking upon the church, chosen by Christ to be his bride, adorned with his love, and protected by his power, the daughters of Jerusalem are astonished and cry, 'Who is this that cometh out of the wilderness like pillars of smoke, perfumed with myrrh and frankincense, with all the powders of the merchant?'

Two things

This question tells us two things about the church of Christ in this world. First, so long as we are in this world the church of Christ is in a wilderness. The Lord's people here are passing through a wilderness, as strangers and pilgrims in a foreign and hostile land. Here we must expect to meet with danger on every hand, trials, tribulations, and temptations.

'Who is this that cometh out of the wilderness?' — The church of God is passing through this wilderness. She is coming up out of it. She has no attachment to it. Believing men and women must take care never to live for this world. We simply must not entangle ourselves with the affairs of this world. To love this world is to be the enemy of God (James 4:4; 1 John 2:15; Matt. 6:31-33).

Second, as the people of God make their way through this world their hearts are set upon another world. The church is said to be 'like pillars of smoke, perfumed with myrrh and frankincense'. Her heart is inflamed with love for Christ. Her affections are set upon things above, not on the perishing things of the world (Col. 3:1-3; 2 Cor. 4:18). The graces of the Spirit in the believer's heart are like sweet spices and holy incense, arising from the altar of the renewed soul's heart.

Matthew Henry wrote, 'The graces and comforts with which she is perfumed are called 'the powders of the merchant,' for they are far fetched and dearly bought by our Lord Jesus, that blessed Merchant, who took a long voyage and was at vast expense, no less than that of his own blood, to purchase them for us. They are not products of our own soil, nor the growth of our own country; no, they are imported from the heavenly Canaan, the better country.'

Christ's Presence

The primary thing revealed in this passage is this. While the church is in this world she is with Christ and Christ is with her, and she is safe. All is well! Sometimes our doubting hearts become fearful about the welfare and safety of the Lord's church. But our fears are ill-founded. The church belongs to Christ. He loved her, chose her, and redeemed her. She is in his hands. He will defend her, protect her, and perfect her. The church of Christ and the cause of Christ are safe.

> Zion stands by hills surrounded,
> Zion kept by power Divine;
> All her foes shall be confounded,
> Though the world in arms combine:
> Happy Zion, what a favoured lot is thine!
>
> Every human tie may perish;
> Friend to friend unfaithful prove;
> Mothers cease their own to cherish;
> Heaven and earth at last remove;
> But no changes can attend Jehovah's love!
>
> Zion's Friend in nothing alters,
> Though all others may and do;
> His is love that never falters,
> Always to its object true.
> Happy Zion, crowned with mercies ever new!
>
> If thy God should show displeasure,
> 'Tis to save and not destroy;
> If he punish, 'tis in measure,
> 'Tis to rid thee of alloy.
> Be thou patient; soon thy grief shall turn to joy.

In the furnace God may prove thee,
Thence to bring thee forth more bright;
But can never cease to love thee;
Thou art precious in his sight;
God is with thee, God thine everlasting light.

Daughters of Jerusalem

'The daughters of Jerusalem' seem to be representative either of our younger brothers and sisters in Christ (Those who truly are converted, but still just babes in grace), or of those who only profess to be converted, but are yet lost, blind, and ignorant. Perhaps both. These daughters of Jerusalem stand admiring the bride, the church, and commending her; but she overlooks their praises and points them to her Beloved. She transfers all the glory to Christ. The church would have all to look away from her to Christ. We applaud and praise him. We recommend him to your esteem. Christ alone is worthy of praise. He alone is worthy of notice.

She calls him Solomon, but the One spoken of is Christ. 'Behold, greater than Solomon is here!' Solomon was a type of Christ. Both are the sons of David and the sons of God, kings of peace over the house of God. Solomon was a type of Christ, in his wealth and wisdom, in the greatness and peacefulness of his kingdom, in his marriage to the daughter of Pharaoh[2], and in building the temple. In these verses the church expresses her admiration and praise for Christ in three ways: 1. The safety of his bed (vv. 7-8); 2. The splendour of his chariot (vv. 9-10); 3. The greatness of his person (v. 11).

The safety of his bed

Here the church admires and praises Christ because of the safety of his bed (vv. 7-8). 'Behold his bed, which is Solomon's; three-score valiant men are about it, of the valiant of Israel. They all hold swords, being expert in war: every man hath his sword upon his thigh because of fear in the night.'

She calls for the daughters of Jerusalem to, 'Behold his bed', look to him and trust him, because there is safety in him. The church is his bed. He said of it, 'This is my rest for ever; here will I dwell.' The believer's heart is his bed. He lies all night between our breasts, and reveals his love in our hearts (Eph. 3:17). Heaven is his bed, the rest into which he entered when he had finished his work.

But here 'his bed' refers to that rest and satisfaction which believing hearts find in communion with Christ. When we are nestled in his arms in sweet communion and fellowship, we find rest and peace for our souls. Here is a bed long enough and broad enough for a man to stretch himself upon. The bed upon which we rest is Christ himself! The covers of this bed (our Lord's own righteousness!) are infinitely broad, broad enough for the biggest sinner in the world to wrap himself in! It is a green, fruitful bed (1:16). It is my bed (3:1). And it is his bed (3:7). The bed he bought. The bed he owns. The bed he gives. The bed he is!

In particular, the bride is safe and secure because the Lord has posted guards about his bed to protect her. Travelling through this wilderness in the darkness of night, the people of God are always subject to danger, being susceptible to attacks at all times. But we have no need to fear. The cause of Christ is safe in this world. The Lord himself protects his people. And he has set his angels to protect his saints. But we have something more tangible than this.

C. H. Spurgeon said, 'Our gracious God has been pleased to commit unto men the ministry of Christ. The Lord ordaineth that chosen men should be the protectors of his church; not that they have any power of themselves to do anything, but he girdeth the weak with strength and maketh the feeble mighty; so then, men, even the sons of men stand in array…to guard both the bridegroom and the bride.'

It is the responsibility of those who preach the gospel to be watchmen, caring for and protecting the church of God. Faithful pastors are angels of the churches to guard them and watch over them (Heb. 13:7, 17; Rev. 1:20). Read verses seven and eight care-fully, and you will notice that there are always enough swordsmen for the work.

'Threescore valiant men' — There are always enough men cho-sen of God for the deliverance of his people and the protection of his church. 'The Lord gave the Word, and great was the company of them that published it.' There shall always be just as many faith-ful pastors to carry on the battle, as the battle shall require (Gen. 19:16). The Lord knows who they are, where they are, where they are needed, and what he will use them to accomplish.

These warriors were men of the right mettle, 'the valiant of Israel'. The servants of God are men, bold and fearless men, men with a cause to inspire them and courage to carry them through. Valiant men are dependable men, courageous men, devoted men, and proved men.

These men were all in the right place. 'Threescore valiant men ABOUT IT.' There were some on the right, some on the left, some in the front, some in the rear. Each man was in the place where God had put him. Each man was in the place where he was need-ed and for which he was gifted. Each man kept his post.

These sixty valiant men were all well armed. 'They all hold swords.' Every valiant warrior in Christ's Israel holds the Sword of the Spirit, the Word of God. The only weapon of our warfare is the Word of God. God's servants carry no other, need no other, and use no other.

Again, these valiant men, chosen of God for the safety of his church, are well trained. 'They all hold swords, being expert in war.' They are all men of war. They had been tried and proved again and again. These men were not academy cadets. They were seasoned veterans. Those who are set apart for the work of the gospel ministry must not be novices. They must be well-trained, well-equipped men (1 Tim. 3:1-7). The church of Christ does not need any 'preacher boys' any more than the U. S. Marine Corps needs 'soldier boys'. We need men to stand as watchmen over Zion — men who have endured trial — men who have proved their faithfulness — men who have an insight into the human heart

— men who are burdened for the cause of Christ — men who
have a sound knowledge of gospel doctrine (Jer. 3:13) — men
who are gifted for the work — men who can preach and preach
with persuasive power and understanding.

These valiant men were always ready. Every man had his
sword upon his thigh and his hand upon his sword. With Paul,
every man called of God to the work will cry, 'I am ready to preach
the gospel!'

The reason for the Lord's appointment of his soldiers is to secure the welfare of his church. They stand at their post 'because of
fear in the night'. They are appointed to their posts to protect her
from any real danger, to comfort her and silence her fears about
supposed danger, and to light her path and guide her through the
dark wilderness.

The splendour of his chariot

Next, the church here expresses her admiration and praise toward
Christ because of the splendour of his chariot (vv. 9-10). 'King Solomon made himself a chariot of the wood of Lebanon. He made
the pillars thereof of silver, the bottom thereof of gold, the covering of it of purple, the midst thereof being paved with love, for the
daughters of Jerusalem.'

As the bed speaks of the believer's communion and fellowship
with Christ in the blessed gospel-rest of faith, the chariot speaks of
the everlasting gospel of Christ. 'The doctrines of the gospel are
comparable, for their antiquity, for their sweet fragrance, for their
incorruptibility, to the wood of Lebanon. The gospel of Christ never decays; Jesus Christ is the same yesterday, today, and forever.
Not one single truth bears any sign of rot. And to those souls who
are enlightened from above, the gospel gives forth a fragrance far
richer than the wood of Lebanon' (C. H. Spurgeon).

The gospel of the grace of God is that chariot in which Christ
reveals himself in this world. The gospel is that chariot in which
Christ our King rides forth conquering and to conquer. And the

gospel of grace is the chariot in which the church of God is carried through this world. It is a chariot the Lord made by his own hands. He devised it and established it. He made it for himself. He made it for his church whom he determined to save. Look at the details of this blessed gospel chariot. Its splendour reflects the glory of our King, its Maker.

The four silver pillars that hold up the canopy of this chariot are the attributes of God himself. The great atonement of Christ, beneath which we are sheltered from the terrible wrath of God, is supported and buttressed by the attributes of God. The divine attributes, God's character, guarantee the efficacy of Christ's atonement.

There stands the silver pillar of God's justice. God cannot and will not slay any soul that is sheltered beneath the blood of Christ. Justice will not allow it. If Christ paid the debt for us, justice cannot demand payment from us. There stands the solid, silver pillar of God's power. We are kept in the hands of Omnipotence. There stands the silver pillar of God's immutable, everlasting love. His love for us is strong and everlasting, unchanging, and eternal. It is as strong as his power and as sure as his justice. His love for us secures our souls. And there stands the silver pillar of God's immutability. Oh, what a pillar this is. The Lord our God changes not. And since he changes not, our souls are safe and secure (Mal. 3:6; Eccles. 3:14).

The purple canopy, or covering of this chariot, is the atonement of Christ. It is dyed in the purple blood of our royal King, which he shed to redeem us at Calvary. That blood-red canopy of finished atonement shelters our souls from the burning heat of the day and the terror of the night. We are sheltered safe and secure under the efficacious, sin-atoning, saving blood of the Lord Jesus Christ. Precious beyond imagination is that blood!

The bottom of this blessed gospel chariot is made of gold, the solid, enduring gold of God's eternal purpose and decree (Rom. 8:28-30; 9:16-18).

Then there is the pavement of needlework. The soft cushions upon which we are made to rest our souls are most delightful. This blessed gospel chariot is paved with Christ's special love for his own elect. 'The midst thereof being paved with love for the daughters of Jerusalem.' That love was the basis of his eternal decree. That love is revealed in his atoning sacrifice. That love is manifest in his constant, unfailing, daily care.

The greatness of his person

Third, the church here admires and praises Christ, because of the greatness of his person (v. 11). 'Go forth, O ye daughters of Zion, and behold king Solomon with the crown wherewith his mother crowned him in the day of his espousals, and in the day of the gladness of his heart.'

Let every sinner who trusts Christ as his Saviour recognize that he is part of the Lord's church, inside the gospel chariot. Yet, looking upon ourselves as one of the daughters of Jerusalem, 'Go forth, O ye daughters of Zion, and behold King Solomon with the crown wherewith his mother crowned him in the day of his espousals, and in the day of the gladness of heart.'

We see the dishonour put upon him by the religious world in his own day. They counted him the off-scouring of the earth and crucified him with glee! We see all around us the dishonour put upon him by the apostate church of this day. His deity is denied by multitudes who profess to be his disciples. His blood is counted a common, useless thing, incapable of saving power and efficacy without the aid of man! His grace is despised as something he merely offers to men, something that may be accepted or rejected by the whim of a fallen man's will!

Let us ever behold the crowns and honours God the Father has put upon our blessed Saviour. He has given him dominion over all things. He has made our all-glorious Christ Lord over all, put all things under his feet, given all judgement to the Son, and made him pre-eminent over all things and the fulness of all things.

Behold, too, the honours put upon the Lord Jesus by his church, by all true believers, in whose heart he is formed, and of whom he said, 'These are my mother' (Matt. 12:50). When we come to Christ in faith, receiving him as our Lord and Saviour, it is a great privilege of grace for us; but it is more. Christ is honoured by it. True faith is honouring to the Son of God. Faith crowns him whom the triune God has crowned.

The day a sinner believes on the Son of God is his coronation day as King in our souls. True faith acknowledges and submits to Christ as Lord and King (Luke 14:25-33). It also is the day of his espousals. He joins us to him in faith and love, and he betroths all that he is and has to us (Hosea 3:3). The day his chosen is brought to him in faith is the day of the gladness of his heart. There is joy in heaven, in the presence of the angels when a sinner trusts Christ. He sees with satisfaction and delight of the travail of his soul (Luke 15:6-8, 10). Let us ever go forth and behold the greatness of Christ's grace toward sinners. This is his crown. This is his brightest diadem of glory!

11.

Christ's own estimate of his church

Song of Solomon 4:1-15

'Behold, thou art fair, my love; behold, thou art fair; thou hast doves' eyes within thy locks...Thou hast ravished my heart, my sister, my spouse; thou hast ravished my heart with one of thine eyes, with one chain of thy neck. '

Remember, the Song of Solomon is to be interpreted spiritually, as an allegory. Any attempt to interpret the book in a strictly literal way is a great mistake, and must lead to very great evil. This is a love song, not between a man and a woman, but between Christ and his bride, the church. It speaks of the intimate relationship and loving communion that exists between the Lord Jesus Christ and his believing people. This Song expresses the affection of a believing heart for Christ and the affection of Christ's heart for his believing people.

One clear indication that the Song must be interpreted as an allegory is found in verse 9. —'Thou hast ravished my heart, my sister, my spouse; thou hast ravished my heart with one of thine eyes, with one chain of thy neck.' Here the church is spoken of as both Christ's sister and his spouse. It would be atrocious to think that Solomon had taken his sister to be his bride! But Christ's church is to him both a sister, and a spouse, and a mother (Matt. 12:50).

The church is called his sister because he took upon himself our nature in the incarnation, and he makes us partakers of his nature in regeneration. He clothed himself with a body (Heb. 2:14), and he clothes the believer with his Spirit (1 Cor. 6:17). Christ owns his church and loves us as his sister, because we are the children of God his Father. Both he that sanctifies and they who are sanctified are all of one (Heb. 2:11).

There is also a marriage-covenant between the Lord Jesus Christ and every believing soul. All true believers are members of the church, which is his bride. We are the bride; he is the Bridegroom. We are espoused to Christ; and he is espoused to us. We are wed to him; and he is wed to us. We are no more two, but one. We are bone of his bone and flesh of his flesh. We are members of Christ himself.

Nothing more beautifully describes our relationship to Christ and our love for him than the love of a bride for her husband. And nothing more beautifully describes our Saviour's love for us than the love of a true husband to his bride. In chapter 3, the church, the bride, spoke lovingly and admirably of Christ, expressing the love and esteem of every believing heart for the Lord Jesus Christ. Now, in 4:1-15, the Lord Jesus Christ speaks lovingly and admirably of his church, expressing his love and esteem for every true believer.

These fifteen verses show us Christ's own estimate of his church. A loving wife does not find her joy and comfort in what her friends and neighbours may think of her. And she does not find joy and comfort in what she thinks of herself. If she truly loves and reverences her husband, she will always think herself to be an unworthy wife. But she finds all her joy and comfort as a wife in her husband's high opinion of her. If her husband loves her and honours her above all women, in his thoughts, in his speech, and in his conduct, she is happy. She desires no more than this. Even so, the true believer finds no joy and comfort in the opinions of others about him, or in his own opinions about himself. But if he can be persuaded that the Lord Jesus Christ holds him in the high esteem of love and honour, there he finds all the comfort and joy his heart can crave. In this passage the Lord Jesus declares to every believer that he holds us in the highest possible esteem of perfect love.

If you are a child of God, a believer, the Lord Jesus Christ, the Son of God, here assures you that he holds you in such great esteem and honour that his very heart is ravished by you! He says, 'Thou hast ravished my heart, my sister, my spouse; thou hast ravished my heart with one of thine eyes, with one chain of thy neck!' What an amazing statement!

Perfect in beauty

Here is the first thing to be learned from this chapter. It is a lesson that we are all very reluctant to learn; but once learned, it is most comforting to our hearts. The Lord Jesus Christ declares that his church is perfect in beauty (vv. 1-7):

> Behold, thou art fair, my love; behold, thou art fair; thou hast doves' eyes within thy locks: thy hair is as a flock of goats, that appear from mount Gilead. Thy teeth are like a flock of sheep that are even shorn, which came up from the washing; whereof every one bear twins, and none is barren among them. Thy lips are like a thread of scarlet, and thy speech is comely: thy temples are like a piece of a pomegranate within thy locks. Thy neck is like the tower of David builded for an armoury, whereon there hang a thousand bucklers, all shields of mighty men. Thy two breasts are like two young roes that are twins, which feed among the lilies. Until the day break, and the shadows flee away, I will get me to the mountain of myrrh, and to the hill of frankincense. Thou art all fair, my love; there is no spot in thee.

By nature there is no beauty in us. There is nothing about us to commend us to the love of God. We are all black, unclean, and corrupt by nature. Both at heart and in outward appearance, we are evil. In our own esteem, there is nothing beautiful in us. The more we know Christ, the more we know ourselves. And the more we know ourselves, the more hideous we appear in our own eyes. Who are we that he should look upon us with favour?

But in the eyes of Christ we are perfect in beauty. Three times he declares, 'Behold, thou art fair, my love, behold, thou art fair... Thou art all fair, my love: there is no spot in thee!' In him and in his eyes, we are complete, we are beautiful, and we are perfect. Christ has made us perfect and beautiful in every detail! (Ezek. 16:8-14; Eph. 5:25-27). He has thoroughly removed every spot of sin from us. He has taken away our sins and has implanted a new nature within us (1 John 3:5-9). He will soon present us to himself faultless before his Father's throne in his own perfection (Col. 1:21-22; Jude 24-25). The Lord Jesus describes his church as having a sevenfold beauty. In his eyes, everything about her is perfect! 'Behold, thou art fair, my love; behold, thou art fair...'

1. 'Thou hast doves' eyes within thy locks.' The bride's eyes are as peaceful 'doves' eyes.' The eyes of her understanding are enlightened. The eye of faith by which believers look to Christ are singular, looking to him alone for salvation. We look to him alone for acceptance with God, righteousness, pardon, and eternal life.

2. 'Thy hair is as a flock of goats, that appear from mount Gilead.' Our Saviour observes and is concerned with the most minute details of our lives (Matt. 10:30). As a woman's hair is her glory and is used in Scripture to symbolize her subjection to her husband (1 Cor. 11:6-15), so the Lord Jesus looks upon the believer's willing subjection to him as a matter of great beauty in his eyes.

3. 'Thy teeth are like a flock of sheep that are even shorn, which came up from the washing; whereof every one bear twins, and none is barren among them.' Sheep have teeth that are white and harmless. They are not ravenous, harmful creatures, but both peaceful and clean. As such their teeth are used here to speak of

both the peacefulness and the cleanness of God's saints, being washed in the blood of Christ.

4. 'Thy lips are like a thread of scarlet, and thy speech is comely.' John Gill's comments on this sentence are excellent. 'As lips are the instruments of speech, the words of the church, and of all true believers, may be designed. What is said by them in their prayers, which are filled, not with great swelling words of vanity, exalting themselves, and magnifying their works, like the Pharisee; but with humble confessions of sin, and acknowledgments of their unworthiness of mercy. They are constant, like one continued thread, they go on praying all their days. The scarlet colour may denote the fervency of them, whereby they avail with God, and the acceptableness of them to God, through the mediation of Christ, whose blood, and not any worthiness of theirs, is pleaded in them. Their words of praise also may be signified hereby; which are filled with expressions of the goodness and grace of God to them, and with thankfulness for all mercies, both temporal and spiritual, bestowed upon them. These are hearty and sincere, coming from a heart inflamed with the love of God, which make such lips look like scarlet; and that being in great esteem may intimate the acceptableness of them to God, through the blood and sacrifice of Christ.'

5. 'Thy temples are like a piece of a pomegranate within thy locks.' Pomegranate must be cut open to see its beauty and fruitfulness. When cut open, it displays rows of seeds and bursts with a reddish liquid. Our Lord uses it to speak of the beauty of his church. Her beauty and fruitfulness is not on the surface, but within. It is not that which men behold and admire; but that which he beholds and admires. Yet, as the pomegranate is full of reddish liquid within, so God's people blush with shame before him because we know what we are by nature.

6. 'Thy neck is like the tower of David builded for an armoury, whereon there hang a thousand bucklers, all shields of mighty

men.' In beautiful contrast to the blushing temples, the Saviour beholds the neck of his bride and compares it to an erect tower of David. It is not the stiff neck of unbroken pride (Isa. 48:4; Acts 7:51), or the burdened neck of legal bondage (Lam. 1:14; Acts 15:10), but the erect neck of gospel freedom in Christ (Isa. 52:2).

7. 'Thy two breasts are like two young roes that are twins, which feed among the lilies. Until the day break, and the shadows flee away, I will get me to the mountain of myrrh, and to the hill of frankincense. Thou art all fair, my love; there is no spot in thee.' Poetic language is often passionate. Here, as the impassioned lover attempts to describe the beauty of his bride, language fails him. The comparisons, obviously, are not strictly correct. The intent is to show how utterly beautiful she is in his sight. Still, the two breasts of the bride may (as John Gill, John Trapp, and others suggest) refer to the Old and New Testaments, which are twins, in perfect harmony and full.

The Lord Jesus Christ is so pleased with the beauty of his Church that he has chosen her to be his rest forever (v. 6). —'Until the day break, and the shadows flee away, I will get me to the mountain of myrrh, and to the hill of frankincense.'—'The LORD thy God in the midst of thee is mighty; he will save, he will rejoice over thee with joy; he will rest in his love, he will joy over thee with singing' (Zeph. 3:17).

A call to communion

Second, our blessed Saviour calls us to walk with him in sweet fellowship and communion (v. 8). 'Come with me from Lebanon, my spouse, with me from Lebanon: look from the top of Amana, from the top of Shenir and Hermon, from the lions' dens, from the mountains of the leopards.' Here he gives us a gracious call to come along with him as a faithful Bride, to come away from our own people and our father's house, and to cleave only to him.

This is a precept we must obey — 'Come with Me.' All who have come to Christ by faith must come with Christ in holy communion. Being joined to him, we must walk with him. We must come with Christ away from all the pleasant mountains of this world. Matthew Henry wrote, 'This is Christ's call to his spouse to come off from the world, all its products, all its pleasures, to sit loose all the delights of sense. All those must do so that would come to Christ. They must take this affections off from present things.' Child of God, we who belong to Christ must look beyond this world. We must live above the perishing things of time. We must set our hearts upon Christ (2 Cor. 4:18; Col. 3:1-3). We who belong to the Son of God live above the dangers of this world, let us also live above the cares of this world. But this eighth verse is much more than a precept for us to obey.

This is also a promise we should enjoy. Christ's church shall be brought home with him to heaven. We shall be delivered in due time from all the dangers and difficulties of this world. Soon, the lions of hell and the leopards of darkness will torment us no more! 'The God of peace shall bruise Satan under your feet shortly' (Rom. 16:20).

Ravished with love

Third, we are told that Christ's very heart is ravished with love for his people (vv. 9-15):

> Thou hast ravished my heart, my sister, my spouse; thou hast ravished my heart with one of thine eyes, with one chain of thy neck. How fair is thy love, my sister, my spouse! how much better is thy love than wine! and the smell of thine ointments than all spices! Thy lips, O my spouse, drop as the honeycomb: honey and milk are under thy tongue; and the smell of thy garments is like the smell of Lebanon. A garden enclosed is my sister, my spouse; a spring shut up, a fountain sealed. Thy plants are an or-

chard of pomegranates, with pleasant fruits; camphire, with spikenard, Spikenard and saffron; calamus and cinnamon, with all trees of frankincense; myrrh and aloes, with all the chief spices: A fountain of gardens, a well of living waters, and streams from Lebanon.

The Lord Jesus Christ has made us so perfectly beautiful in his sight that he is ravished with love for us! The love of Christ for us is the real affection of his heart. The God-man loves us. The Son of God so loves us that he delights in us! The Lord Jesus Christ is ravished with our love for him (1 John 4:19). The love we have for him is a love he has created and given us. Yet, it is truly ours. 'We love him because he first loved us.' But we do love him. We did not, would not, and could not love him by nature. But now he has put such a love in our hearts for him that he is ravished by it. His love for us precedes our love for him eternally. His love for us exceeds our love for him infinitely. And his love for us caused our love for him effectually. But we do love him sincerely.

The Son of God, our all-glorious Christ is ravished by the grace that he has put upon us. 'The smell of thine ointments.' The fruit of the Spirit created in us and the graces of the Spirit wrought in us are a sweet aroma to our Redeemer. They are a sweet smelling ointment to him, because they are his gifts to us, the gifts of his own grace (Gal. 5:22-23; Ezek. 16:9-14).

Our blessed Saviour is ravished by our speech, too, because it is all about him. 'Thy lips'. The most delightful and most constant theme of a loving Bride is her Husband. And the believer's most joyful speech is about Christ. Those who know Christ love to speak of him. We love to speak of who he is, what he has done, why he did it, where he is now, what he is doing there, and when he shall return.

Looking into our hearts, the Lord Jesus Christ is ravished by our thoughts of him. 'Honey and milk are under thy tongue.' He hears our thoughts. He knows those precious thoughts we have of him, thought that words can never express.

Knowing the sincerity of our hearts, the Lord Jesus Christ is ravished by our works performed for him. 'The smell of thy garments.' Without question, these garments are the garments of salvation that he has wrought and bought for us, which he brought to us, and put upon us:

- Garments of Imputed Righteousness
- Garments of Imparted Righteousness
- Garments of Grace and Holiness

Yet, the church of Christ is a garden flourishing with good works, works done for him, works that he has created in us (vv. 12-15). She is a garden planted by his grace and watered by his Spirit, so thoroughly and effectually watered that she has become herself a fragrant, fruitful fountain of gardens and living waters, with streams flowing out of her into all the world to refresh the earth. That is the picture drawn in verses 12-15:

A garden enclosed is my sister, my spouse; a spring shut up, a fountain sealed. Thy plants are an orchard of pomegranates, with pleasant fruits; camphire, with spikenard, Spikenard and saffron; calamus and cinnamon, with all trees of frankincense; myrrh and aloes, with all the chief spices: A fountain of gardens, a well of living waters, and streams from Lebanon.

Our works, the works of God's church, those works performed for Christ are never counted by us as being worthy of anything. We know that if we did all things perfectly, we would only have done what we should have done. We constantly repent even of our best, noblest, most righteous works, because 'all our righteousnesses are filthy rags' before the holy Lord God. But he whom we love and serve looks upon our puny works as his pleasant fruits. They are rich, sweet fragrances, the smell of which ravishes his heart. They are works of faith and love. They are works produced by him and honoured by him (Eph. 2:10). That which is done by faith in Christ, arising from a heart of love for him, are honoured and accepted by him. Let us ever rest in his love, walk in communion with him. And let us faithfully serve our Redeemer, who loved us and gave himself for us.

12.

My heart—his garden

Song of Solomon 4:16

'Awake, O north wind; and come, thou south; blow upon my garden, that the spices thereof may flow out. Let my beloved come into his garden, and eat his pleasant fruits.'

Here, as in many places in the Holy Scripture, the believer's heart is compared to a fruitful garden. If we are the Lord's people, if there is true faith in us, our hearts are the Lord's garden. Each believer's heart is a garden he has purchased, a garden he has enclosed, a garden he has tilled, a garden he has planted and watered. The believing heart is a garden that belongs to Christ and brings forth many pleasant fruits for him. Here the beloved bride speaks to her beloved Lord and expresses her hearts desire. 'Awake, O north wind; and come, thou south; blow upon my garden, that the spices thereof may flow out. Let my beloved come into his garden, and eat his pleasant fruits.'

What a difference there is between what we are by nature and what we have been made by the grace of God! By nature we are like a barren wilderness, or an empty desert. But now, by the grace of God, we who believe have been transformed into fruitful gardens. Our wilderness is made like Eden. Our desert has been turned into the garden of the Lord. We have been enclosed by grace. We have been tilled and sown by the hand of God. Our

Lord said to his disciples, 'My Father is the husbandman.' Now the Divine Husbandman has made us fruitful to his praise. Where there was once no fruit and nothing to give him delight, he now comes to 'eat his pleasant fruits'. Grace makes a great change (2 Cor. 5:17).

In the parable of the sower our Lord compares us to a garden. In a garden, flowers and fruits and vegetables are planted and cultivated with purpose and care. And in every true believer's heart you will find evidences of the cultivation and care of the Divine Gardener. In the good ground, mentioned in the parable, some of the seed brought forth thirty-fold, some sixty-fold, and some a hundred-fold. It is true, not all of the Lord's gardens are precisely the same in their productivity. Some yield more, and some yield less fruit. Still, every garden brings forth its fruit and flowers in measure to the honour and glory of God.

A fruitful garden

Our hearts are here compared to a fruitful garden. The believing heart is Christ's fruitful garden. Our hearts are the Lord's garden; and they bring forth fruit, both for his honour and for his pleasure. There is no such thing as a barren, fruitless, graceless believer. Wherever true grace is found in the heart, there will be the fruit of grace.

The believer's heart is a garden into which the good seed of the gospel has been sown (Matt. 13:18-23). It is that ground made good and fruitful by the grace of God. No ground is naturally good. It naturally brings forth weeds, briars, and thistles. Before the ground is fit to receive seed, it must be prepared. A wise and good farmer takes much care in properly preparing his ground before he sows his seed. As the farmer sows his seed, some may fall upon the rocks, some by the wayside, and some among thorns. But only that ground which is thoroughly prepared will receive the seed and bring forth fruit.

How does a farmer prepare his ground? He purchases the ground, plows the field, encloses the field, sows the seed, waters the ground, and cultivates the tender plant. In precisely this way the Lord Jesus Christ, like a wise husbandman, has made the hearts of his people his fruitful garden. He purchased us with the price of his own precious blood. He has enclosed us, marking our hearts and souls as his own peculiar property. We were enclosed by his decree of election. We were enclosed by the hand of his wise and gracious providence. He has ploughed the field of our hearts, thoroughly breaking up the fallow ground of our hearts, by conviction. He has planted the good seed of the gospel in our hearts, enabling us to hear and understand the blessed word of grace. He waters the ground of our hearts by his grace. He cultivates the tender plants of his garden with trials and afflictions.

Not only are our hearts his garden, every heart that belongs to Christ is a fruitful garden (Gal. 5:22-23). In the new birth God the Holy Spirit comes into a man's heart in sovereign, life-giving power. And where the Spirit of God comes there is fruit. The Spirit of the Lord brings life, abundant, productive life (2 Cor. 5:17).

'The fruit of the spirit'

The produce of the Lord's garden is 'the fruit of the Spirit', not the works of our own hands. The believer's graces are not character-istics, or moral virtues, which he produces by diligence and care. These things are the fruits of the Spirit, inevitable results of his grace and power.

Notice that Paul speaks of 'the fruit of the Spirit' as one. He names many virtues; but they are all one. They are like a cluster of grapes. They are many; yet, in essence, they are all one. They all spring from one Vine; and that Vine is Christ himself. All who are really and truly connected to the Vine bear the fruit of the vine (John 15:1-6).

Notice, also, that Paul, when he talks about the fruit of the Spirit, speaks of attitudes, not actions. He tells us that if a person is truly born of God, his inward heart attitude will reflect it. God regards not the actions of men but the attitudes of their hearts. Human religion may change a man's actions. But the grace of God changes the attitude of the heart. Hypocrites reform their actions. Believers undergo a mighty renewing of the heart.

In every believing heart these three clusters of fruit are found. I do not suggest that every believer has this fruit in the same measure. But I do say that every true believer has this pleasant fruit in its essence. In one it is as the newly sown seed. In another it is like a tender plant. In another it is like an ear of corn, not yet full. In another it is like the fully ripe ear, ready for harvest. But in all the essence is the same.

'The fruit of the Spirit is love, joy, peace.'

This describes our relationship to God. Our relationship to the Lord our God is not one of dread, and fear, and anxiety. We walk before him in love, joy, and peace. This describes our marvellously free, open fellowship with the Lord God. Believers love the Lord. We love his Word, his will, his ways, his worship, and his people. We rejoice in the Lord, as well as love him. We rejoice in his person, his purpose, his providence, and his salvation. And we are at peace with God.

'The fruit of the Spirit is Longsuffering, gentleness, goodness.'

This describes our relationship and attitude toward those around us. The children of God are not hard, critical, and severe. They are patient, gentle, and good to the people around them. True faith is patient, both with providence and with people. True faith is gentle:

courteous, thoughtful, and kind. True faith is manifest by goodness toward men: generosity, openness, simplicity, and understanding.

'The fruit of the Spirit is faith, meekness, temperance.'

This describes the true believer's inward character. It tells us what the people of God truly are. They are faithful, honest, and dependable. Believers are meek. Knowing who they are and whose they are, they are truly and honestly humble in their own eyes. And faith in Christ makes people temperate. The children of God are men and women who control their passions. They are modest and temperate in all things. Temperance is control from within. By the grace of God, believers control their tempers, their lusts, and their appetites.

These things are not the result of our labours of self-discipline and self-denial. These things are the result and outflow of God's grace in regeneration. This is the fruit of the Spirit. It is simply the overflowing of the Spirit of grace in the renewed heart (John 7:37-38).

I am constrained to ask this question. 'Is my heart truly the Lord's garden?' Am I truly one of the Lord's own children? Let us each honestly examine ourselves in this matter. A truly renewed heart is fruitful. It brings forth the fruit of the Spirit. Let us quit looking at our actions and our experiences. We all must honestly face this question: Is my heart a fruitful garden to the Lord?

Heavenly wind

Our garden and its fruit need the Breath of Heaven. 'Awake, O north wind; and come, thou south; blow upon my garden that the spices thereof may flow out.'

Sometimes, though the flowers are in bloom their sweet fragrance does not fill the air, because there is no gentle breeze to carry it about. One may walk in the garden where spices abound and never smell their rich odours if there is no wind stirring. Therefore, the loved one of our text prays that the Breath of Heaven might come and break the dead calm of her heart's garden so that the rich fragrance of her spices might flow forth.

In this prayer there is an evident sense of inward sleep — 'Awake, O north wind.' This is a poetic confession that she herself needs to be awakened. Her appeal is to the Spirit of God, the great Breath of Heaven, who operates according to his own will, even as 'the wind bloweth where it listeth'. She does not try to raise the wind, and create a revival in her own heart. She simply acknowledges her utter dependence upon God the Holy Spirit to awaken her graces and enliven her heart.

If the Spirit of the Lord will blow upon our garden, our spices will flow out. Let him move upon us as he will, from the north or from the south. He knows best. If he will but move upon us, our hearts will respond. Sometimes he revives our hearts with the chilling, rough wind of affliction. Sometimes he revives us with the gentle southern breeze of grace and mercy. Sometimes he uses both the cold winds of the north and the gentle breezes of the south to stir us. This is the thing we need. We wait for a visitation from the blessed Spirit of God. If the Breath of Heaven will blow upon us, the fragrant flowers of our garden will fill the air with their rich perfume.

Come and eat

'Let my beloved come into his garden and eat his pleasant fruits.' We greatly desire that the Lord himself will visit his garden. The bride does not desire for the spices of her garden to fill the air with their fragrance for her own enjoyment, nor even for the delight of the daughters of Jerusalem. Her desire is that her spices may flow forth for the pleasure and enjoyment of her Beloved.

The highest, noblest wish of our souls is that Christ may have joy, pleasure, and delight in us. And the great condescension of grace is this: The Lord Jesus Christ, the Son of God, our great Saviour, does delight and take pleasure in his people.

She calls him hers — 'My beloved'. What music there is in these two words. He is 'My beloved'. My graces, the flowers of my garden, may be terribly dormant. But he is my Beloved still. With these words we acknowledge that we belong to Christ. My heart is his garden. The fruit and affection of my heart belongs to him, only to him.

This is the prayer and desire of our hearts. 'Let my beloved come.' Let him come in the glory of his second advent. Let him come in the majesty of his judgement-seat. Let him come to make all things new. But, let him come into my heart!—'Let him come into his garden, and eat his pleasant fruits.' Child of God, open your heart to the King of Heaven, our great Solomon, and he will come. He will sup with you; and you will sup with him (Rev. 3:20).

13.

Christ present with his church

Song of Solomon 5:1

'I am come into my garden, my sister, my spouse: I have gathered my myrrh with my spice; I have eaten my honeycomb with my honey; I have drunk my wine with my milk: eat, O friends; drink, yea, drink abundantly, O beloved.'

In the preceding verse we see the church, the bride of Christ, making a twofold prayer. First, she asked for the gracious influence of the Holy Spirit. 'Awake, O north wind; and come, thou south; blow upon my garden that the spices thereof may flow out.' Then, she asked for the manifest presence of Christ himself. 'Let my beloved come into his garden, and eat his pleasant fruits.'

Here we have the Lord's gracious answer to that prayer. Here the Lord Jesus Christ himself speaks and says, 'I am come into my garden, my sister, my spouse: I have gathered my myrrh with my spice; I have eaten my honeycomb with my honey; I have drunk my wine with my milk: eat, O friends; drink, yea, drink abundantly, O beloved.'

Here our Lord Jesus speaks of his manifest presence with his church. We should not be greatly surprised to hear him speak in such a manner. Did he not say that if any would open to him he would come in and sup with them (Rev. 3:20)? Our all-glorious Christ is always as good as his promise. No sooner did his church throw open the doors of her heart than he entered and made himself known in sweet communion.

Of this one thing we may be sure. Every heart that is prepared by God to receive Christ, and anxiously seeks and desires the presence of Christ shall have Christ (Isa. 65:24). Certainly this is true with regard to poor, needy sinners (Heb. 4:16). This is most assuredly true with regard to you who are the Lord's.

The fact that our hearts truly long for Christ's presence is evidence that he is with us already. Sometimes we are like Jacob when he awoke out of his sleep, he said, 'Surely, the Lord is in this place and I knew it not.' We are often like Mary; on one occasion the Lord was standing by her side in the garden, and she knew him not. George Burrowes wrote, 'The fact of the existence of such desires for him, is evidence of his being with us; as in this passage, in immediate connection with the request, he adds, "I have already come." He was present in the heart, though his presence was not felt.'

Christ's presence

The Lord Jesus Christ calls for us to take notice of his presence. Our prayer in the last verse of chapter four was, 'Let my beloved come into his garden.' Here he says, 'I have come into my garden', as if to say, 'Look up, my beloved, I am here!' Could it be that he has come without us perceiving it? Could he be present and us, who so earnestly long for him, not know it? I am afraid that it is so. Our hearts are so much taken up with doubt and worldly concern that unless Christ advertises his coming, as he does here, he might be at our side and us fail to see him.

A local church is the gathering of two or three needy souls in the Name of Christ. Our Master promised that where two or three gathered together in his Name, he would be present with them (Matt. 18:20). The place in which his people gather is not important. The number present is not important. The denominational name is not important. The only matter of importance is that we gather in his Name.

But what does it mean to gather in his Name? To gather in his Name is to gather believing on his Name, trusting him alone as our Mediator and Saviour. To gather in his Name is to come together to worship him and seek his glory. To gather in his Name is to come together seeking his righteousness, his will, his mercy, and the salvation of his sheep.

Our Saviour has promised to be with his people, those who truly worship him in Spirit and in truth, at all times (Isa. 43:1-3; Matt. 28:18-20). He said, 'I will never leave thee, nor forsake thee' (Heb. 13:4). And our Lord Jesus Christ has promised his manifest presence to those who love him (John 14:18-23). This is the thing I am talking about. We know the doctrine of Christ's presence. But we want to know his real, manifest presence with us. Wherever the door is opened to Christ, he comes in (Rev. 3:20). Wherever there is a heart broken and contrite before God, Christ takes up his abode in that heart (Isa. 57:15; 66:1-2).

This personal, manifest presence of Christ among his people is an unspeakable blessing of grace. When our Lord is manifestly present in our assemblies there is life in our midst, fervency in our prayers, vitality in our songs, and blessedness in hearing his voice as his Word is read. The preaching of the gospel is the delivery of a message from God and the hearing of it is the hearing of a message from God. When he is absent, all is lifeless and dead. When He is present there is joy and peace in Jerusalem. Any who miss Christ, miss him because they will not seek him.

Christ's satisfaction

Our dear Saviour is ever present with his church because he finds great satisfaction in his church. His church is not a building, or a denomination. His church is his people. All true believers, considered collectively, are his church. And the Son of God finds great satisfaction in his people. He says to his church, 'I am come into my garden, my sister, my spouse: I have gathered my myrrh with my spice; I have eaten my honeycomb with my honey; I have drunk my wine with my milk.'

Here our Lord claims the church as his own garden, his rightful possession. In this one verse he uses the personal possessive pronoun 'my' nine times. Certainly this is meaningful. We rightfully belong to the Lord Jesus Christ. We are his by divine gift in eternal election (John 6:39), by lawful purchase in particular redemption (1 Cor. 6:19-20), and by omnipotent, effectual grace in regeneration (Ezek. 16:8).

The sweet produce, which Christ finds in his garden, is the result of his own cultivation. He takes pleasure in us just as a farmer takes pleasure in his fruitful field. He finds satisfaction in us just as a mother finds satisfaction in her living, healthy baby.

Without question, our Lord's language in this place is designed to convey to us the message that he finds great satisfaction and delight in his people. What condescending grace! The Son of God comes to us! But that is not all; he even looks upon us with complacency, delight, and satisfaction! Because of his own blood and righteousness, he accepts the sincere, though feeble, worship of our hearts (1 Pet. 2:5). Our offerings are to him like the gathering of his myrrh and spice. Our prayers are like sweet-smelling myrrh to him. Our songs of praise are like spices and incense before him. Our love toward him is like honey in the honeycomb to our Redeemer. Our joy before him is like exhilarating wine. Our daily lives are like refreshing milk to him! Imagine that.

In this heavenly poetic verse, Christ is fed first, then his children are invited to eat. It seems to imply that our first concern should be for him. The first and best of everything must go to him.

Christ's invitation

The Son of God gives a loving invitation to his beloved people. He says, 'Eat, O friends; drink, yea, drink abundantly, O beloved.' He calls us to a feast of fellowship, communion, and life. It is spread not for the world, but for his own peculiar people.

Notice the two words by which he tenderly calls us to the feast: 'friends' and 'beloved'. He calls us his friends (John 3:29; 15:13-15; Luke 15:7). We were by nature his enemies. And we would have forever remained his enemies. But he has graciously reconciled us to himself. We are his friends! He calls us his beloved. All who are born of God are the peculiar objects of his great love — Electing Love! — Redeeming Love! — Immutable, Unchanging Love! — Saving Love! — Preserving Love! Oh, what blessedness is heaped up in that word as it falls from our Saviour's lips, 'Beloved!'

Notice the two provisions for our souls to feast upon. We are bidden to eat and drink. You know what the food of faith is, and what the delightful drink is. The food and the drink are in him. By faith, we eat his flesh and drink his blood (John 6:50-56). That is to say, we live by constantly trusting his righteousness and obedience unto death as our sin-atoning Substitute.

Notice this delightful word, too, — 'abundantly'. Our Lord tells us to feast abundantly upon him. Let faith eat and drink, feeding upon Christ without end. The more your hunger and thirst is satisfied, the more you will hunger and thirst. —Feast on! This is healthy gluttony. The marginal translation of this last phrase is, 'Be drunken with loves.' It is as though the Lord is saying, 'Come, my friends, my beloved, drink the rich wine of my love, until your heart is drunk with my love, until you are totally under the influence of my love' (Eph. 5:18).

There is never any danger of overindulgence when it comes to preaching, feeding upon, and worshipping the Lord Jesus Christ. Oh, child of God, gorge your self on Christ! Drink of him, O my soul, until you are thoroughly, completely intoxicated with him, and then drink on!

14.

'I sleep, but my heart waketh'

Song of Solomon 5:2-8

'I sleep, but my heart waketh: it is the voice of my beloved that knocketh, saying, Open to me, my sister, my love, my dove, my undefiled: for my head is filled with dew, and my locks with the drops of the night. I have put off my coat; how shall I put it on? I have washed my feet; how shall I defile them? My beloved put in his hand by the hole of the door, and my bowels were moved for him. I rose up to open to my beloved; and my hands dropped with myrrh, and my fingers with sweet smelling myrrh, upon the handles of the lock. I opened to my beloved; but my beloved had withdrawn himself, and was gone: my soul failed when he spake: I sought him, but I could not find him; I called him, but he gave me no answer. The watchmen that went about the city found me, they smote me, they wounded me; the keepers of the walls took away my veil from me. I charge you, O daughters of Jerusalem, if ye find my beloved, that ye tell him, that I am sick of love.'

What a sad but common story! Here is the church of Christ, his beloved, chosen, and redeemed bride in her most lamentable condition. She is slothful, negligent, and indifferent. In other places the bride speaks to Christ, but here she speaks of him, because now he had withdrawn himself.

Oh, yes, he is always with us. He will never leave us, nor forsake us. How we ought to thank God for that blessed fact. His mercy is everlasting! His love is immutable! His grace is indestructible! But he does sometimes, for our souls' good, hide himself and appears to have forsaken us altogether. We are, at times, compelled to cry out with David, 'My God, my God, Why has thou forsaken me? Why art thou so far from helping me, and from the words of my roaring?'

When that is the case, when our fellowship and communion with Christ is broken, because of our base ingratitude, neglect, and indifference, the only remedy is that the Lord himself graciously return to us and revive our hearts according to his own sovereign pleasure.

How often we are compelled to speak as the church speaks in this place, 'I sleep, but my heart waketh!' Sometimes this cold, this deathly indifference steals over only one or two hearts in a congregation. Sometimes it seems to engulf entire assemblies. Sometimes this black plague seems to engulf the whole church of Christ. It is an experience with which I am afraid we are all too familiar. We all know by bitter experience the deep base notes of Newton's hymn:

How tedious and tasteless the hours
when Jesus no longer I see!
Sweet prospects, sweet birds, and sweet flowers,
have all lost their sweetness to me.
The mid-summer sun shines but dim;
the fields strive in vain to look gay;
But when I am happy in him,
December's as pleasant as May.

His Name yields the richest perfume,
and sweeter than music his voice;
His presence disperses my gloom,
and makes all within me rejoice:
I should, were he always thus nigh,

have nothing to wish or to fear;
No mortal so happy as I;
my summer would last all the year.

Content with beholding his face,
my all to his pleasure resigned,
No changes of season or place
would make any change in my mind;
While blest with a sense of his love,
a palace a toy would appear;
And prisons would palaces prove,
if Jesus would dwell with me there.

Dear Lord, if indeed I am thine,
if thou art my sun and my song,
Say, why do I languish and pine,
and why are my winters so long?
Oh, drive these dark clouds from my sky,
thy soul cheering presence restore;
Or take me unto thee on high,
where winter and clouds are no more.

There is within each of us a terrible tendency to become neglectful, indifferent, and lukewarm towards the Lord Jesus Christ. This common, sinful tendency of our nature must be marked, acknowledged and avoided.

Prone to wander, Lord, I feel it,
prone to leave the God I love:
Here's my heart, Oh, take and seal it,
seal it for thy courts above.

'I sleep.'

Here is a very common sin. 'I sleep.' The wise virgins often sleep with the foolish. Far too often this is the bad effect great privileges have upon our sinful hearts. When we indulge ourselves in carnal ease and security, our hearts become cold, neglectful, drowsy, and indifferent. Prayer becomes a burden. Devotion languishes. Worship sinks to nothing more than bodily exercise. Zeal dies.

'But my heart waketh!'

Here is a hopeful sign. 'But my heart waketh.' It is a hopeful sign that there is grace in the heart when the heart struggles against that horrid, sinful sluggishness to which we are so prone. Ours is not the sleep of death. There is life within, struggling, struggling hard against sin (Rom. 7:14-22). 'It is the voice of my beloved.'

Here is a very loving and tender call. 'It is the voice of my beloved.' All is not gone. Though my heart sleeps so foolishly, yet Christ is my Beloved. Though my love is so fickle, so shameful, and so unworthy of him, I do love him. And what is more, I still hear his voice and know his voice.

The Lord Jesus Christ tenderly knocks to awaken us to come and open to him (Rev. 3:20). By his Word, by his providence, and by his Spirit, the Son of God knocks at the heart's door of his beloved, because he will not be spurned by the object of his love. He will not leave his own. Neither will he let his own leave him. He has betrothed us unto himself forever (Hos. 2:19).

He not only knocks for entrance. Our beloved Redeemer graciously calls us, wooing us to himself by his grace. Whose voice is it? 'It is the voice of my beloved that knocketh.' Who is he calling? 'My Sister!' 'My Love!' My Dove!' 'My Undefiled!' What does he call for? 'Open to me.' Why is he calling? 'My head is filled with dew, and my locks with the drops of the night' the night of his agony in Gethsemane, in the judgement hall, when he was crowned with thorns, piercing his brow.

'I have put off my coat!'

Here is a most ungrateful excuse. 'I have put off my coat; how shall I put it on? I have washed my feet; how shall I defile them?' (v. 3). Because of her carnal ease, she refused the Lord's gracious invitation to communion. She did not want to trouble herself, and she did not want to be troubled, not even by him! Her heart was so cold that she preferred her ease to the fellowship of Christ. Let us be honest. We are often so wrapped up in worldly care and carnal ease that we become almost, if not altogether, indifferent to our Lord Jesus Christ!

'My Beloved put in his hand!'

But our Lord is gracious still. Our Redeemer's love cannot be quenched. He is longsuffering, patient, and gracious to his people, even in our most sinful rejection and denial of him. Here is a picture of our Saviour's persevering, effectual grace. 'My beloved put in his hand by the hole of the door, and my bowels were moved for him' (v. 4). It is written, 'Thy people shall be willing in the day of thy power, in the beauties of holiness from the womb of the morning: thou hast the dew of thy youth' (Psa. 110:3). How our hearts rejoice to know that Christ will not leave his people to themselves. As the hymn writer put it, 'He will never, never leave us, nor will let us quite leave him!' His grace is effectual. His grace is persevering. His grace is irresistible. His grace is preserving. Yes, his grace is indestructible! He knocks; but we are so cold, so indifferent, so hard that we would never open to him.

'My Beloved had withdrawn himself!'

Here is a sad picture of the loving chastisement our neglect and indifference brings upon us. 'I rose up to open to my beloved; and my hands dropped with myrrh, and my fingers with sweet smelling myrrh, upon the handles of the lock. I opened to my beloved; but my beloved had withdrawn himself, and was gone: my soul failed when he spake: I sought him, but I could not find him; I called him, but he gave me no answer. The watchmen that went about the city found me, they smote me, they wounded me; the keepers of the walls took away my veil from me' (vv. 5-7; Isa. 54:9-10). Thank God for faithful watchmen who will not allow us to hide behind any veil, excusing our indifference and sin, but faithfully expose us to ourselves and point us to Christ for mercy and grace!

'If ye find my beloved...'

Here is one last hope. 'I charge you, O daughters of Jerusalem, if ye find my beloved, that ye tell him, that I am sick of love' (v. 8). She could not find Christ for herself, so she employed the help and assistance of the Lord's people.

Cherish the precious fellowship of Christ. Let nothing rob you of your rich privilege. Do nothing to drive him away (Eph. 4:30). But when you have grieved the Spirit of God, when the Lord Jesus hides his face from you, do not despair. It is not because he has ceased to cherish you (1 John 2:1-2), but because he cherishes you so much that he is determined to make you pine for him. Are you sick of love? Does your soul long for fresh tokens of Christ's love to you? When your soul languishes, child of God, when sin robs you of Christ's manifest presence and sweet communion, as soon as he calls, open to him. 'Today, if ye will hear his voice harden not your heart.' Go back to the cross. Confess your sinful negligence. Go on seeking him. Trust him still (2 Sam. 23:5; Lam. 3:18-33).

Return, O Son of God return!
Come knock again upon my door.
Dear Saviour, my Beloved, return.
Possess me and depart no more!

15.

Let me tell you about my beloved

Song of Solomon 5:9-16

'*What is thy beloved more than another beloved, O thou fairest among women? what is thy beloved more than another beloved, that thou dost so charge us? My beloved is white and ruddy, the chiefest among ten thousand. His head is as the most fine gold, his locks are bushy, and black as a raven. His eyes are as the eyes of doves by the rivers of waters, washed with milk, and fitly set. His cheeks are as a bed of spices, as sweet flowers: his lips like lilies, dropping sweet smelling myrrh. His hands are as gold rings set with the beryl: his belly is as bright ivory overlaid with sapphires. His legs are as pillars of marble, set upon sockets of fine gold: his countenance is as Lebanon, excellent as the cedars. His mouth is most sweet: yea, he is altogether lovely. This is my beloved, and this is my friend, O daughters of Jerusalem.*'

Let me tell you about my Beloved. His Name is Jesus Christ, the Lord. He is my Saviour, my Redeemer, my Prophet, my Priest, my King, and my All. He is my Lord; and he is my God. But he is more — Jesus Christ is the Beloved One of my heart and the Friend of my soul. He is 'the chiefest among ten thousand', and 'he is altogether lovely'.

Has God the Holy Spirit created in your heart a desire to know him. This is the thing that matters. Christ is the one thing needful.

It is not enough that we know about Christ. We must know Christ. It is not enough that we know the doctrine of Christ. We must know Christ himself. It is not enough that we merely know about Christ crucified on the tree, we must know the crucified Christ in our hearts. To that end, let me tell you about him. All beauty, excellence, and perfection, divine and human, dwells in the Lord Jesus Christ. He is the perfect God and the perfect man. All that our souls need and all that will satisfy our hearts is found in Christ in infinite abundance.

The context

In verses 2-8 the Lord came to bless his church (his bride, his beloved) with his presence, his fellowship, and his communion (v. 2). But he found his church asleep, slothful and negligent. He was shamefully treated with neglect (v. 3). He graciously caused her to desire him, creating in her heart a longing for his presence (v. 4). Then the Lord withdrew himself from her (v. 5-6). It was not at all his desire to punish her. He simply intended to cause her to see his preciousness to her. So, in order to make her properly value and esteem him, the Lord withdrew and hid himself from her for a while. At last we see the church, the bride of Christ, his beloved, holding him to be precious. When she had lost the sense of his presence, she saw how valuable and necessary he was to her soul. And she gave this solemn charge to those who were around her: 'I charge you, O daughters of Jerusalem, if ye find my beloved, that ye tell him, that I am sick of love.'

The question

'What is thy beloved more than another beloved, O thou fairest among women? what is thy beloved more than another beloved, that thou dost so charge us?' (v. 9). There is hope for men when they begin to inquire about the beauty, the perfection, the excellence, the grace, and the glory of Christ. 'What is thy beloved more than another beloved?' That is a question believing souls delight to answer. Yet, it is a question that I can never answer fully.

The answer

'My beloved is…' How can he be described? Someone wrote,

> What the hand is to the lute,
> What breath is to the flute,
> What fragrance is to the smell,
> What the spring is to the well,
> What the flower is to the bee,
> That is Jesus Christ to me.
>
> What the mother is to the child,
> What the compass is in pathless wild,
> What oil is to the troubled wave,
> What ransom is to the slave,
> What water is to the sea,
> That is Jesus Christ to me.

His character

The question is raised, 'What is thy beloved more than another beloved?' Here is a general description of his character: 'My beloved is white and ruddy, the chiefest among ten thousand' (v. 10). My Beloved is one of incomparable perfection, unparalleled beauty, and infinite excellence. He is so infinitely precious above all others that he alone is Precious. His loveliness is so infinitely higher than the loveliness of others that he alone is Lovely.

He has everything in himself that is pleasant, lovely, and admirable. 'He is white and ruddy.' These words refer to the excellence of his divine glory as God and the excellence of his mediatorial character as man. In him resides all the perfection of the eternal God. And in him is all that our souls need. He is the holy, immaculate, eternal Son of God. And he is made unto me wisdom, and righteousness, and sanctification, and redemption. His love toward me makes him lovely to me. He is white in the spotless innocence of his life, and ruddy in the bloody sufferings of his death. He is white in his glory as God, and ruddy[1] in his incarnation as man. He is white in his tenderness toward his people, and ruddy in his terrible vengeance upon his enemies.

My Beloved is so infinitely above all others that there is none to compare with him. 'He is the chiefest among ten thousand.' In comparison with Christ, every other object of love and affection is but dung (Phil. 3:8). He is higher than the kings of the earth; and he has obtained a more excellent name than any in heaven, or earth, or hell (Ps. 89:27; Heb. 1:4; Phil. 2:9-11).

In his church, Christ is the Chief Corner-Stone. Among the brethren Christ is the Firstborn. Among the resurrected Christ is the First-Begotten. He is the Alpha and the Omega. He is the Firstborn of every creature. God has made Christ to be pre-eminent in all things. And in the hearts of his people, He is pre-eminent (Col. 1:14-20). The marginal translation says, 'He is the Standard-Bearer among ten thousand.' He is lifted up as the Ensign, to whom his people gather. He is lifted up as the Banner, around whom we rally (Isa. 11:10; John 12:32).

The question is asked, 'What is thy beloved more than another beloved?' The bride answers, 'My beloved is white and ruddy, the chiefest among ten thousand.' But that is not enough. A more detailed description must be given of him who ravishes her heart. She wants all to know how she beholds him — Excellent in Beauty! — Omnipotent! — Gracious! — In every way worthy of her trust! — Fully qualified to redeem and save his people and bring them all, at last, safe to heaven! Christ is worthy of our love, our trust, and our highest admiration and esteem. He is so transcendently glorious that he is both great and gracious.

His head

'His head is as the most fine gold' (v. 11). His head speaks of our Lord's sovereign dominion over all things (Eph. 1:22). Like gold, the sovereignty of Christ is beautiful, strong, and precious. All who know this great King relish the fact that he is indeed King over all!

His hair

'His locks are bushy, and black as a raven' (v. 11). His hair is at the same time white and black. Whiteness denotes his eternality and wisdom (Rev. 1:14). Blackness speaks of his perpetual strength and power.

His eyes

'His eyes are as the eyes of doves by the rivers of waters, washed with milk and fitly set' (v. 12). His eyes are pure. His eyes toward us are peaceable. His eyes are penetrating. His eyes are powerful, irresistible. One look of his eye struck Peter's heart. His eyes never blink. They are always fixed upon the objects of his love.

His cheeks

'His cheeks are a bed of spices, as sweet flowers' (v. 13). The very sight of his face, like a rich, fragrant garden, is reviving, refreshing, and pleasing.

His lips

'His lips are like lilies, dropping sweet-smelling myrrh' (v. 13). His lips are so sweet and pleasant. The words of his lips are sweeter than honey and the honeycomb. The kisses of his lips are better than wine. Grace is poured into his lips. And grace proceeds out of his lips. Grace poured out of his lips as our Surety when he pledged himself to the salvation of his chosen. Grace poured out of his lips as our Substitute at Calvary, when he said, 'Father, forgive them!' and cried again in triumphant majesty, 'It is finished.' Grace pours from his lips as our Saviour. He comes to his own in the time of love, spreads over his redeemed the skirt of his righteousness, and says, 'Live!' He declares, 'I have loved thee with an everlasting love, therefore with lovingkindness have I drawn thee.'

His hands

'His hands are as gold rings set with beryl' (v. 14). His hands, like golden rings, fitted to the finger, are fitted to accomplish their purpose —the salvation of his people (Matt. 1:21). His hands, like the king's signet, seal the covenant of God's grace. The piercing of his hands in death was the ratification of God's covenant.

His heart

'His belly (His bowels of compassion, His heart) is as ivory overlaid with sapphires' (v. 14). The love of Christ's heart for his people is as strong and firm as ivory. The many instances of his love, by which he reveals his love, are as sapphires and precious jewels. Electing Love! Redeeming Love! Life-Giving Love! Preserving Love! Interceding Love! Forgiving Love! Unfailing Love! Faithful Love! Immutable Love! Everlasting Love! His Love! There is none like it! Words can never describe it!

His legs

'His legs are as pillars of marble, set upon sockets of fine gold' (v. 15). He is The Rock! His legs are strong. His legs are stable. In other word, the Lord Jesus Christ is ever dependable. He will never be turned aside from his purpose. And he is able to accomplish it.

His countenance

'His countenance is as Lebanon, excellent as the cedars' (v. 15). In height, in strength, in power, in grace, in beauty, and in love he excels all others. There is none to rival him.

His mouth

'His mouth is most sweet' (v. 16). The words of his mouth are sweet to his people. The precepts of his Word are sweet. The principles of his Word are sweet. The promises of his Word are sweet. The kisses of his mouth, the many tokens of his love and goodness, have a transcendent sweetness in them.

What more can be said? What more can I tell you about my beloved? 'He is altogether lovely!' 'Unto you therefore which believe, He is precious.' He is truly lovely. He is wholly lovely. There is nothing in him but that which is lovely, and there is nothing truly lovely but that which is in him. All that our souls need is in him in infinite fulness (Ps. 73:25-26). Christ is altogether lovely. In his divinity he is lovely. In his humanity he is lovely. In his redemption he is lovely. In his salvation he is lovely. In his providence he is lovely. He is even lovely in his justice and judgement.

The assurance

'This is my beloved, and this is my Friend' (v. 16). Matthew Henry wrote, 'To see Christ, and not to see him as ours, would be rather a torture than a happiness; but to see one that is thus lovely, and to see him as ours, is complete satisfaction.'

It is faith in him that gives this assurance (Heb. 11:1). We know that Christ, in all the fulness of his grace and glory, is ours, because I trust him. Every believing heart has the right to say with Thomas to the Son of God, 'My Lord and my God.' He is ours in all of his offices. He is ours in all of his works. He is ours in all of his ways. He is ours in all of his provisions. He is ours always, both now and forever. He is ours in all his possessions. He is ours, both when he openly reveals himself, and when he hides his face; both when we sense it and when we do not, he is ours. In prosperity and in adversity, in health and in sickness, in joy and in sorrow, Jesus Christ is mine, and I am his.

Because Christ is ours, he is our Beloved. He loves us and we love him (1 John 4:19). He is our one true love. We have chosen him. We have willingly, deliberately given ourselves to him. Our hearts are for him, only him, and not another.

And Jesus Christ the Lord, our Beloved is our Friend. O what a Friend! He is a powerful Friend. He is a sympathetic Friend. He is a patient Friend. He is an unchanging Friend. He is a wise Friend. He is a faithful Friend. He is my Friend. I have done what I can to tell you about my Beloved. I do not know whether you will ever trust him or not; but he is worthy of your trust. I do not know whether you will ever love him or not; but he is worthy of your love. I do not know whether you will ever praise him or not; but he is worthy of your praise.

16.

'This is my friend'

Song of Solomon 5:16

'His mouth is most sweet: yea, he is altogether lovely. This is my beloved, and this is my friend, O daughters of Jerusalem.'

I've found a Friend, O such a Friend!
He loved me ere I knew him;
He drew me with the cords of love,
and thus he bound me to him.
I've found a Friend, O such a Friend!
He bled and died to save me;
And not alone the gift of life, but his own self he gave me.

I've found a Friend, O such a Friend!
All power to him is given
To guard me on my onward course,
and bring me safe to heaven.
I've found a Friend, O such a Friend!
So kind and true and tender,
So wise a counselor and guide, so mighty a Defender!

The Lord Jesus Christ, the Son of God, is the Friend of needy sinners. Someone once said, 'Friendship is the only thing in the world concerning the usefulness of which all mankind are agreed.'

A friend is one of the greatest blessings on earth. Affection is far better than gold. Sympathy is indescribably better than property. The poorest man in all the world is the man who is friendless and alone. If you would be happy in this world, you must have friends. And if you desire happiness in eternity, you must find a Friend in Jesus Christ, the Son of God, the only Saviour of poor sinners.

The world is full of sorrow, because it is full of sin. It is a dark place. It is a lonely place. It is a disappointing place. The brightest sunbeam in this dark world is a friend. A friend will make our sorrows half what they would otherwise be. And a friend doubles every joy. But a real friend is a scarce and rare treasure. Many will share the bright sunshine of happiness and prosperity. Few will weep with us when we weep and stand by our sides in the dark night of adversity. The sick, the helpless, and the poor find that friends are scarce indeed. Above all, there are few who will care for our souls!

The friendship of this world is as bitter as it is brittle. Trust in it, and you will have trusted a robber. Rely upon it, and you will have leaned upon a spear that will pierce your soul. The Lord Jesus Christ is a real Friend, an everlasting Friend, and a Friend in *every* time of need. Christ is the Friend we need.

The sinner's friend

The Lord Jesus Christ is the Friend of sinners, the only true Friend sinners have. He made it his common practice to eat with publicans and sinners, so much so that he was commonly derided as the 'friend of publicans and sinners' (Matt. 9:10-13; 11:19). But that which his enemies thought was his shame is his glory. The Son of God came into this world specifically on an errand of mercy, love, and grace. He came into the world to save sinners. He lived for sinners. He died for sinners. He rose again for sinners. He intercedes for sinners. He loves sinners. He saves sinners (Rom. 5:6-8).

The sinner's faithful friend

The Lord Jesus Christ is the 'friend that sticketh closer than a brother' (Pro. 18:24). On a purely earthly level, Solomon tells us that if we would have friends, we must show ourselves friendly. 'A man that hath friends must show himself friendly.'

I have never known an obviously friendly person who did not have an abundance of friends. If we would have people be thoughtful of us, we must be thoughtful of others. If we would have kindness shown to us, we must be kind to others. If we want people to speak well of us, we must speak well of others. If we want people to be generous toward us, we must be generous to others.

I have observed that usually those who are most easily offended are those who think nothing of offending. Those who complain the most about doing things are those who always do as little as they can without public embarrassment. Those who are the most selfish are those who complain most about the selfishness of others. Those who are the most unfriendly are the very ones who complain that others are unfriendly. 'A man that hath friends must show himself friendly.'

Look at the next line of Proverbs 18:24. Solomon tells us, 'There is a friend that sticketh closer than a brother.' He did not find this Friend in his unbridled pleasures, or in the wanderings of his unlimited research, but in the pavilion of the Most High, in the secret dwelling place of the Almighty, in the Person of the Lord Jesus Christ. I can tell you, both from the Word of God and from the experience of more than thirty-five years, that our all glorious Christ, my Lord, my God, my Redeemer, my Saviour, is the greatest, best, wisest, most loving, disinterested, and faithful of Friends. How happy is that family whose family Friend is Jesus Christ! How happy and blessed is that man whose best Friend is the Son of God! 'There is a Friend that sticketh closer than a brother,' and his name is Immanuel, the Christ of God. 'This is my beloved, and this is my friend.' I have never been much of a friend to him; but, oh, what a Friend he is to me!

Poor, weak, and worthless, though I am,
I have a rich, almighty Friend;
Jesus, the Saviour, is his Name:
He freely loves, and without end.

He ransomed me from hell with blood;
and by his power my foes controlled:
He found me wandering far from God,
and brought me to his chosen fold.

He cheers my heart, my wants supplies,
and says that I shall shortly be
Enthroned with him above the skies:
Oh! What a Friend is Christ to me!

But, oh! My inmost spirit mourns;
and well my eyes with tears may swim,
To think of my perverse returns:
I've been a faithless friend to him.

Sure, were I not most vile and base,
I could not thus my Friend requite:
And, were he not the God of grace,
He'd frown and spurn me from his sight!

The friend needed

The Lord Jesus Christ is the one Friend we need. Yes, the Son of
God is a Friend to sinners in need. And man is the most needy
creature on God's earth, because he is a sinner. There is no need
so great as that of sinners. Poverty, hunger, thirst, cold, sickness, all
are nothing in comparison with sin.

As sinners, we need righteousness; but we have no power to
get it. We need atonement; but we have no ability to make it. We

need pardon; and we are utterly unable to provide it for ourselves. We need deliverance from a guilty conscience and the fear of death; but we have no power in ourselves to obtain it.

Christ, is a Friend to sinners in need. He came into the world to relieve us of the great need caused by sin. He came to remove our guilt, save us from sin, and deliver us from the curse of the law. It was said of the child Jesus, 'Thou shalt call his name Jesus, for he shall save his people from their sins' (Matt. 1:21). 'This is a faithful saying, worthy of all acceptation, Christ Jesus came into the world to save sinners, of whom I am chief!' (1 Tim. 1:15). Let me show you from the Word of God why we need Christ as our Friend.

All of us by nature are poor, diseased, dying creatures

From the President in the White House, to the farmer in the field, from the professor at the University, to the school-boy in kindergarten, we are all sick from the mortal disease of the soul — sin. Whether we know it or not, whether we feel it or not, we are all dying because of sin. We are as

> a sinful nation, a people laden with iniquity, a seed of evil doers, children that are corrupters: we have forsaken the Lord, we have provoked the Holy One of Israel unto anger, we are gone away backward...the whole head is sick, and the whole heart faint. From the soul of the foot even unto the head there is no soundness in us; but wounds, and bruises, and putrifying sores: they have not been closed, neither bound up, neither mollified with ointment (Isa. 1:4-6).

The plague of sin is in our hearts. 'The heart is deceitful above all things, and desperately wicked: who can know it?' (Jer. 17:9). 'God saw that the wickedness of man was great in the earth, and that every imagination of the thoughts of his heart was only evil continually' (Gen. 6:5). 'Out of the heart proceed evil thoughts, murders, adulteries, fornications, thefts, false witnesses, blasphemies: These are the things which defile a man' (Matt. 15:19-20).

Our problem is that we have a heart disease, a disease incurable, except by the blood of Christ and his almighty grace. The root of all sin is in your heart and mine by nature. It is the heart that must be changed. We must have a new heart implanted within us. Christ alone can change the sinner's heart. This plague of the heart has so permeated our being that every faculty of man, both body and soul, is defiled with sin:

> We have before proved both Jews and Gentiles, that we are all under sin; as it is written, There is none righteous, no, not one: there is none that understandeth, there is none that seeketh after God. We are all gone out of the way, we are together become unprofitable; there is none that doeth good, no, not one. Our throat is an open sepulchre: with our tongues we have used deceit; the poison of asps is under our lips: our mouth is full of cursing and bitterness: Our feet are swift to shed blood: Destruction and misery are in our ways: and the way of peace have we not known: There is no fear of God before our eyes. Now we know that what things so ever the law saith, it saith to them who are under the law: that every mouth may be stopped, and all the world may become guilty before God...For all have sinned, and come short of the glory of God (Rom. 3:9-19, 23).

Our understanding is so perverse that we will never seek God. Our throats are so corrupt that they are like open graves. Our tongues are deceitful weapons. Our lips are full of poisonous words. Our mouths are but vehicles to express anger, bitterness, and wrath. Our feet run to do evil. Our ways are full of misery and end in destruction. Our eyes look to do evil, having no fear of God.

These things are not true of a few, very wicked and openly vile people. They are true of us all. We are all, at the very core of our beings, abominably wicked and totally depraved. There are no exceptions. This disease of sin, this plague of the heart, is an inbred, family disease, passed on from father to son, generation after generation. It is a disease that grows worse and worse, with every passing hour.

Christ alone can cure our souls of the disease of sin. We could never cure ourselves. No angel or man could produce a remedy for sin. But the Lord Jesus Christ came into the world to cure us of the plague of the heart. 'Behold, I will bring it health and cure, and I will cure them, and reveal unto them the abundance of peace and truth' (Jer. 33:6). He came 'to abolish death, and bring life and immortality to light through the gospel' (1 Tim. 1:10).

All of us by nature are debtors to God

We were bankrupt sinners, head over heels in debt to the Almighty. We owed our God ten thousand talents, and had not one penny with which to pay. We could never have freed ourselves from the debt of sin; but only got more deeply involved day after day. The Lord Jesus Christ came to pay our debt. He cancelled the bill, paying the full requirements of God's holy law. Jesus paid it all, all the debt I owed! O my soul, how I ought to love him! There is not a soul out of hell whose debt was so great as mine (Lk. 7:40-43).

All of us by nature were under the curse of the law

The sentence was upon us. 'The soul that sinneth, it shall die.' We could never satisfy the demands of the law. We could not keep its precepts. We could not appease its wrath. We could not atone for sin. But Jesus Christ came to do for us what we could never do for ourselves. He kept the precepts of the law as our Representative before God. He died under the curse of the law as our Substitute, putting away sin.

'Christ hath redeemed us from the curse of the law, being made a curse for us, for it is written, Cursed is everyone that hangeth on a tree' (Gal. 3:13). 'Who his own self bare our sins in his own body on the tree, that we, being dead to sins, should live unto righteousness: by whose stripes ye were healed' (1 Pet. 2:24).

All of us by nature were shipwrecked, perishing, and sliding into hell

We could never, in ourselves, have reached the harbour of everlasting life. We were sinking in the midst of the waves, shiftless, hopeless, helpless, and powerless. We were tied and bound by the chain of our sins, in bonds under the burden of guilt, imprisoned under the yoke of the law, and slipping (No! Running headlong!) into hell. All this, our Lord saw and undertook to remove. He came down from heaven to 'proclaim liberty tot he captives, and the opening of the prison to them that are bound' (Isa. 61:1). He came 'to seek and to save that which was lost' (Luke 19:10). He came to 'deliver us from going down into the pit' (Job 33:24).

Yes, the Lord Jesus Christ is a Friend in need. He is the Friend I need and the Friend you need. We could never have been saved without the Lord Jesus Christ coming down from heaven. Salvation would have been an impossibility without Christ. The wisest men of Egypt, Greece, and Rome combined could never have found a way of peace with God. Without the friendship of Christ, we would all have been lost forever in hell. Could we have changed our hearts? Could we have satisfied the demands of the law? Could we have delivered ourselves from the bondage of sin? Could we have paid our debts to God? Could we have delivered ourselves from the jaws of hell? No! No! A thousand times no! Without our Friend, Christ Jesus, we would be forever damned.

It was our Lord's own free love, mercy, and pity that brought him down from heaven to save us. He was in no way obliged to do so. He came and saved us, unsought, unasked, unwanted, because he was gracious, just because he loved us! Search the history of the world. Look around the globe. Examine all of those whom you know and love. There never was such a friend as the Lord Jesus Christ, the Son of God.

> There's not a friend like the lowly Jesus,
> No not one! No not one!
> None else could heal all our souls diseases,
> No not one! No not one!

The Lord Jesus Christ is the only true Friend a sinner has. He is the one Friend who will always be our Friend, the one Friend who sticks closer than a brother. The Son of God is the Friend we need. Sinners can have this Friend unconditionally, forever. He is the Friend of all who trust him. Indeed, he is such a Friend that he takes his worst enemies into his very heart and reconciles their hearts to him, giving them faith, causing them, by the conquest of irresistible mercy, love and grace, to trust and love him. 'This is my Friend!' May God the Holy Spirit make him yours.

17.

Oh, what a friend!

Song of Solomon 5:10-16

'My beloved is white and ruddy, the chiefest among ten thousand. His head is as the most fine gold, his locks are bushy, and black as a raven. His eyes are as the eyes of doves by the rivers of waters, washed with milk, and fitly set. His cheeks are as a bed of spices, as sweet flowers: his lips like lilies, dropping sweet smelling myrrh. His hands are as gold rings set with the beryl: his belly is as bright ivory overlaid with sapphires. His legs are as pillars of marble, set upon sockets of fine gold: his countenance is as Lebanon, excellent as the cedars. His mouth is most sweet: yea, he is altogether lovely. This is my beloved, and this is my friend, O daughters of Jerusalem.'

The wise man, Solomon, tells us that, 'A man that hath friends must show himself friendly.' And I want you to see that there was never a person who showed himself so friendly as the Lord Jesus Christ. We are also told, 'And there is a friend that sticketh closer than a brother.' The Lord Jesus Christ is that Friend. 'This is my beloved, and this is my friend.' What kind of Friend is Jesus Christ? I cannot even begin to describe him. I want to simply set before you some blessed characteristics of the sinner's heavenly Friend. He is the truest Friend a sinner has.

Excellent

Christ is a Friend of transcendent excellence. The Lord Jesus Christ is a Friend who has fully demonstrated his friendship. The true extent of a man's friendship must be measured by his deeds. Do you want a friend indeed? Christ is a Friend in deed. Tell me not what a man says, and feels, and wishes. Tell me not of his words. Tell me rather of what he does. 'Friendly is as friendly does.' The things that our Lord Jesus Christ has done for his people, are the great proofs of his friendship for us.

Suretyship

The Son of God agreed to become our Surety in the Covenant of Grace before the world began (Prov. 6:1-2; Heb. 7:22). When our cause was desperate, he engaged it. When justice was ready to give us the deathblow we deserved, he intervened and absorbed it. When he knew that we would become bankrupt debtors, he became our bondsman, agreeing to pay our whole debt. When he saw that we would fall into the depths of sin and misery, he undertook to bring us out, to cleanse us from all sin, to clothe us in his own righteousness, and to bring us safe to eternal glory. Was there ever such an eternal Friend as Christ? No, not one can compare with him.

Incarnation

For our sakes, the Lord of Glory took into union with himself our nature, and was born of a woman. 'Ye know the grace of our Lord Jesus Christ, who, though he was rich yet for our sakes, he became poor, that we through his poverty might be made rich' (2 Cor. 8:9). For our sakes, the Christ of God lived thirty-three years in this world, despised and rejected of men, a man of sorrows and acquainted with grief. 'He took on himself the form of a servant, and humbled himself' (Phil. 2:7-8).

Substitutionary death

It was for our sakes that the Son of God suffered the painful and shameful death of the cross. 'Greater love hath no man than this, that a man lay down his life for his friends' (John 15:13). Though innocent and without fault, he allowed himself to be condemned and found guilty. Though he was without sin, he was made to be sin for us, that we might be made the righteousness of God in him. He who was the Prince of Life was led as a Lamb to the slaughter. He poured out his soul unto death. He died for us. Behold the Christ of God, dying in your stead. Mark his sighs, his groans, his death, his victory as your Substitute, and relish this blessed claim of faith — 'This is my beloved, and this is my friend!'

Was the Lord Jesus in anyway obliged to die for us? Perish the thought! He might have summoned the help of more than twelve legions of angels, and scattered his enemies with a word. He suffered voluntarily, of his own will and purpose, to make atonement for our sins. He knew that nothing but the sacrifice of himself could satisfy God's law. He knew that nothing but his blood could wash away our sins and make peace between sinful man and the holy Lord God. He laid down his life to pay the price of our redemption. He died that we might live. He bore our shame that we might receive his glory. 'He died the just for the unjust, that he might bring us to God' (1 Pet. 3:18).

O matchless love! Here is unparalleled friendship. 'Greater love hath no man than this, that a man lay down his life for his friends.' But the Christ of God gives even greater evidence of his friendship, 'for when we were enemies, we were reconciled to God by the death of his Son...God commendeth his love toward us in that, while we were yet sinners, Christ died for us.' I ask you, was there ever such a friend who was so high and stooped so low for his friends? Was there ever a friend who gave himself at such a cost in proof of his friendship as Christ? Never was there such a friend in deed as Jesus Christ. Yet, this is not the end of his deeds for us.

Mediation

Christ, our Friend, has also gone to glory to take possession of it in our name, in our room, and in our stead. With his own blood he has obtained eternal redemption for us. In heaven's glory, at the Father's right hand, he intercedes for us unceasingly, as an Advocate with the Father. He presents our services, our sacrifices, and our prayers to the Father, bathed in his precious blood and clothed with the merit of his perfect righteousness (1 Pet. 2:5). He pleads for every blessing we stand in need of. He answers all of Satan's charges against his friends (Rom. 8:33-34).

Powerful

For another thing, the Lord Jesus Christ is a powerful, almighty Friend. There are few in this world who possess the power to help. Many have the will to do others good, but they lack the power. They feel the sorrows of others and would gladly relieve them if they could. They weep with their friends in affliction, but they cannot remove the grief. How helpless we feel to help our friends in their sufferings! We say, 'If there is anything I can do to help', but we know that there is nothing we can do.

Not so with Christ! He is a Friend who is both willing and able to help. Though man is weak, Christ is strong. 'All power in heaven and earth' is given to him. No one can do so much for his friends as Christ. Others can befriend our bodies a little. Christ befriends both body and soul. Others can do a little for us in time. Christ can do everything for us in time and throughout eternity. Let me show you what power there is in this Almighty Friend.

Jesus Christ has the power to pardon and save the very chief of sinners. 'Thou hast given him power over all flesh, that he should give eternal life to as many as thou hast given him. And this is life eternal, that they might know thee the only true God, and Jesus Christ, whom thou hast sent' (John 17:2-3). 'The blood of Jesus Christ, God's Son, cleanseth us from all sin' (1 John 1:7).

Christ has the power to convert the hardest of hearts and create any man anew. 'As many as received him, to them gave he power to become the sons of God, even to them that believe on his name: which were born, not of blood, nor of the will of the flesh, nor of the will of man, but of God' (John 1:12-13). 'If any man be in Christ, he is a new creature: old things are passed away; behold, all things are become new' (2 Cor. 5:17). Christ has power to break the hardest heart and give dead sinners a heart of life. Christ has power to break the most stubborn will and give his chosen a new will. Christ has power to overcome the reigning lusts of men. Christ has power to create us in his own image. Christ has power to give needy sinners repentance and faith. Here is a Friend who has the power to preserve all who trust him unto eternal glory. 'This man, because he continueth ever, hath an unchangeable priesthood. Wherefore he is able also to save them to the uttermost that come unto God by him, seeing he ever liveth to make intercession for them' (Heb. 7:24-25).

And Jesus Christ has the power to give to those who trust him and love him the best of gifts. He gives us life out of death. He gives us peace in adversity. He gives us patience in tribulation. He gives us joy in sorrow. He gives us hope in death. He gives us a crown of glory in eternity. Christ alone is such a powerful Friend. The self-righteous man has no such friend. The legalist has no such friend. The papist has no such friend. The worldling has no such friend.

Love

Again, the Lord Jesus Christ is a loving and affectionate Friend.
Kindness is the very essence of true friendship. Money, advice, and
help lose half their power and value if they are not given in a loving
manner. But this Friend, the Lord Jesus Christ, is a precious Friend,
because his is a 'love that passeth knowledge'.

The love of Christ radiates in his reception of sinners. In love
and mercy our Lord stands before publicans and sinners, tenderly,
affectionately calling them to come to him for life and salvation. It
is the love of Christ that at last conquers our hearts, and wins us
to him. His holiness made us fear. His wrath made us tremble. His
law frightened us away. But his love, that love demonstrated and
commended to us at Calvary, drew our hearts effectually to him.
What love is this? Who can resist this love?

> Oh hope of every contrite heart! Oh joy of all the meek!
> To those who fall, how kind thou art!
> How good to those who seek!
> But what to those who find?
> Ah! This
> Nor tongue nor pen can show;
> The love of Jesus —
> What it is, none but his loved ones know!

Christ never refuses any who come to him in repentance and
faith, seeking mercy. Where can the poor sinner be found who ever
went to Christ, suing for mercy, crying, 'God be merciful to me, I
am the sinner', and found that the gate of mercy refused to open?
There are no bounds to his pity. There is no end to his compassion.
There are no limitations to his mercy. There are no restraints to his
love. In lovingkindness, he says, 'All that the Father giveth me shall
come to me; and him that cometh unto me, I will in no wise cast
out' (John 6:37). Let your sins be as black and vile, abominable
and wretched, as many and varied as they may be, only come to

Christ in faith and you will go away saying, 'Where sin abounded, grace did much more abound.'

Read the gospel narratives again and see how our Lord dealt with sinners in love and pity. There was a woman taken in adultery. The law demanded her punishment. But the Friend of sinners said, 'Neither do I condemn thee, go and sin no more.' There was a harlot who came and washed the Saviour's feet in tears of repentance. The Pharisee was indignant. But Christ was forgiving. There was a Publican named Zacchaeus, who was hated by all around him; but he was befriended, loved, and forgiven by Christ. There was a Samaritan woman, who had five husbands. The disciples marvelled that Christ would stop to talk with such a woman. But he not only talked with her, he gave her the water of life. There was a dying thief who had joined others in railing against Christ. But soon his heart was broken, and in faith he prayed for mercy. To him the Lord promised eternal paradise.

Did ever a sinner meet with so loving a Friend as Christ Jesus? No, never! Churches may shut their doors against you. People may be hardened against you. Preachers may reject you and be repelled by you. But the sinner's one, true Friend will never turn away one who seeks mercy. Go to him. Go directly to Christ, and see if he is not so loving a Friend as I have described.

Yet there is more, the love of Christ is also evident in every aspect of his dealing with sinners after they are converted and become his friends. He is patient with our sins. His ear is always open to our cries. He is our escape in the time of temptation. He is our comfort in the time of trouble. He feels our sorrows and carries our griefs. He supplies our daily needs. He reveals his secrets to us. 'Henceforth I call you not servants; for the servant knoweth not what his lord doeth: but I have called you friends; for all things that I have heard of my Father I have made known unto you' (John 15:15). 'The secret of the Lord is with them that fear him; and he will show them his covenant' (Ps. 25:14).

There is no love in heaven above, or upon the earth beneath that can be compared to the love of Christ, our Friend. He loves us at all times. He loved us before the world began. He loved us when he created us in innocence, after the image of God, in our father Adam. He loved us when we fell in Adam. He loved us when we came forth from the womb speaking lies. He loved us when we hated him. He loved us when we were helpless, ruined, depraved, and dead in sin. He loved us when he called us to life. He loves us in spite of all our sins. He loves us perfectly and immutably. He loves us forever! And the only reason for his love is in himself. He loved us because he would love us! Never, never was there a friend so real, so true, so loving as Christ our Friend.

Wisdom

The Lord Jesus Christ is also a wise and prudent Friend. The friendship of men is sadly blind. We often injure those whom we love by ignorance. We often give our friends bad advice and lead them into trouble, even when we mean to help them. But the friendship of Christ is always wise and prudent. I have but one daughter. And I love her dearly. But I have, at times, spoiled her by extravagance. That is not wise. The Lord Jesus never makes such mistakes in managing the affairs of his friends. Jesus Christ never spoils his friends by extravagant indulgence. Christ gives us all the poverty and all the wealth we need. He gives us all the sickness and all the health we need. He gives us all the sorrow and all the joy we require. He gives us all the pain and all the comfort that is necessary for our good. Like the wise physician, the Lord Jesus mixes our bitterest cups, taking great care that we have not a drop too little, nor a drop too much.

Christ faithfully and wisely rebukes us for our sins. 'Open rebuke is better than secret love. Faithful are the wounds of a friend' (Prov. 27:5-6). The Lord Jesus Christ is a friend whose company is always edifying. His fellowship is always beneficial. One day spent in the company of this heavenly Friend is better than a thousand spent with the best of earthly friends. One hour spent in private communion with Christ is better than a year in kings' palaces. Never was there such a wise and prudent friend as Christ.

Proven

Moreover, the Lord Jesus Christ is a tried and proven Friend. Six thousand years have passed away since the Lord Jesus began his work of befriending mankind. During those six millenniums he has had many friends in this world. Millions have despised this Friend, and are miserably lost forever. But there is an innumerable company of men in heaven and earth who have enjoyed the blessed privilege of Christ's friendship, and have been saved by him. They all testify that Christ is a Proven Friend. Look at the great variety of friends Christ has had and know that there was never a friend like him.

He has had friends of every rank and station in life. Some of them were kings and rich men, like David, Solomon, Hezekiah, and Job. Others were very poor in this world, like the shepherds of Bethlehem, James, John, and Andrew. Christ has had friends of every age known in human history. Some of his friends were very old like Sarah and Abraham, Jacob and Moses. Some of them were but children, like Joseph and Samuel, Josiah and Timothy. Our Lord has had friends of every possible temperament known to man. Some were plain and simple, like Isaac; some were mighty in word and deed, like Moses. Some were fervent, warm-hearted, and fiery, like Peter; others were gentle, shy, and tender, like John. Some were active and stirring, like Martha; others loved to sit quietly at the Saviour's feet, like Mary. Our Saviour has had friends from every possible background and condition. Some were married, like Enoch; others were unmarried, like the Baptist. Some were sick, like Lazarus; others were strong and healthy, like John the Beloved. Some were masters, like Cornelius; others were servants, like Onesimus. Some of them had bad servants, like Elisha; some had bad masters, like Obadiah; and others had bad families,

like David. Some of Christ's friends had been self-righteous Phari-
sees; others had been harlots; one had been a murderer; another
had been a thief. Blessed be God, Christ Jesus stoops down to
rescue the perishing scum and off scouring men of the world and
makes them his friends. Our Redeemer has friends of every nation,
kindred, race, tribe, and tongue in the world.

Go to Adam and Abel, Abraham and Isaac and Jacob, Moses and Joshua, Rahab and Deborah, David and Solomon, Isaiah
and Jeremiah, Peter and John, James and Paul; go to any man or
woman who has tasted that the Lord is gracious, and ask them if
Jesus Christ is not a tried and proven Friend. We stand as one man
and say, 'This is my beloved, and this is my friend', and there is
none like him.

Present

Once more, the Lord Jesus Christ is an unfailing, present Friend.
Perhaps the saddest part of all good things in this world is their
instability. Riches make themselves wings and fly away. Youth and
beauty are but for a few days. Bodily strength soon decays. Mind
and intelligence are soon exhausted. All is perishing. All is fading
away. But there is one blessed exception to this general rule, and
that is the friendship of Jesus Christ.

The Lord Jesus Christ is a Friend who never changes. He is
'the same yesterday, today, and forever' (Heb. 13:8). He says, 'I
am the Lord, I change not; therefore ye sons of Jacob are not
consumed' (Matt. 3:16). Our all-glorious Christ will never leave his
friends. He has promised, 'I will never leave thee nor forsake thee'
(Heb. 13:5). He goes with us wherever we may go. And thus he
fulfils his promise, 'I am with you alway, even unto the end of the
world' (Matt. 28:20).

In our afflictions, Christ is a Friend present to comfort. 'Fear
not: for I have redeemed thee, I have called thee by thy name;
thou art mine. When thou passest through the waters, I will be with
thee; and though the rivers, they shall not overflow thee: when

thou walkest through the fire, thou shalt not be burned; neither shall the flame kindle upon thee' (Isa. 43:1-2). 'Fear thou not; for I am with thee: be not dismayed; for I am thy God: I will strengthen thee; yea, I will help thee; yea, I will uphold thee with the right hand of my righteousness' (Isa. 41:10).

When we are upon the bed of sickness, Christ is the Friend who makes the bed comfortable for us. 'The Lord will strengthen him upon the bed of languishing: thou wilt make all his bed in his sickness' (Ps. 41:3). In death, Jesus Christ is a Friend present to sustain us. 'Yea, though I walk through the valley of the shadow of death, I will fear no evil: for thou art with me; thy rod and thy staff they comfort me' (Ps. 23:4). In the Day of Judgement, Christ will be our Friend in the court of heaven. He will stand by our side in the reckoning day, as an Advocate to plead our cause. When all other friends have failed, Jesus Christ is 'a friend that sticketh closer than a brother'. 'When my father and my mother forsake me, then the Lord will take me up' (Ps. 27:10).

Beloved

Let me show you one more thing, the Lord Jesus Christ is a Friend well-beloved by all who know him. 'Unto you therefore who believe, he is precious.' All who can say in truth and sincerity that Christ is their Friend, will also gladly confess with all of their hearts - 'This is my beloved.' The world thinks that we are fools for making such a confession concerning Christ. They say to us, 'What is thy beloved more than another beloved?' But they have not seen him. They have not known him. They have not embraced him. They have never experienced his grace. They have never known his love. But all who know this divine Friend, rejoice to confess, 'My beloved is white and ruddy, the chiefest among ten thousand...Yea, he is altogether lovely!...This is my beloved, and this is my friend!'

Christ Jesus is a Friend loved by all who know him, because we know who he is. Jesus Christ is a Friend beloved by us, because we have experienced his love. Now, 'we love him, because he first loved us'. The Lord Jesus is a Friend beloved by all who know him, because we know what he has done. Our heavenly Friend is beloved by us, because we know that he is soon coming to receive us.

One there is above all others,
well deserves the name of Friend;
His is love beyond a brother's costly, free, and knows no end:
They who once his kindness prove, find it everlasting love.

Which of all our friends to save us,
could or would have shed their blood?
But our Jesus died to have us reconciled, in him to God:
This was boundless love indeed! Jesus is a Friend in need.

When he lived on earth abased,
Friend of sinners was his Name;
Now above all glory raised, he rejoices in the same.
Still he calls us brethren, friends; and to all our wants attends.

Oh for grace our hearts to soften!
Teach us, Lord, at length to love!
We, alas, forget too often what a Friend we have above:
But when home our souls are brought,
we shall love thee as we ought.

18.

The excellence and supremacy of Christ

Song of Solomon 5:10

'My beloved is white and ruddy, the chiefest among ten thousand.'

The glorious, intimate, loving description of our Lord Jesus Christ given in verses 10-16 is given in response to the question of the daughters of Jerusalem in verse 9. 'What is thy beloved more than another beloved, O thou fairest among women? what is thy beloved more than another beloved, that thou dost so charge us?' In his commentary on the Song of Solomon, Pastor Roger Ellsworth makes a tremendous statement about this:

> The question of the daughters of Jerusalem puts squarely before us a thrilling possibility – it is possible for God's children to so love Christ, and as a result to live in such a way, that they arrest attention and arouse interest. The reverse side of the coin is sombre. It is also possible for God's children to live in such a way that they never stimulate in others any thought about their faith or provoke any consideration of it. The apostle Peter tells his readers to 'Always be ready to give a defence to everyone who asks you a reason for the hope that is in you' (1 Peter 3:15). He expected them to live in such an arresting manner that

they would frequently have to explain why Christ meant so much to them.

May God give us grace to live in such obvious devotion, love, and consecration to Christ that people are aroused to asked us about him.

A question

What a joy it is for a believing sinner to call the Lord Jesus Christ, 'My beloved'. May God give us grace to constantly give him our hearts, to constantly set our hearts' affection upon our Saviour who loved us and gave himself for us (Col. 3:1-3). It is of utmost importance that our hearts' affection be really and truly set upon Christ.

We must trust him; and we must love him. Christ on the cross saves us when he becomes to us as Christ in the heart. It is of little value for us to know about Christ, if we do not really trust him and love him. It is meaningless for us to talk about Christ, unless our hearts are truly wed and knit to him. The orthodoxy of our doctrine is but a mockery of Christ, if we do not love him.

Therefore, I must ask a question. It is a question I ask of myself frequently. 'Is the Lord Jesus Christ my Beloved?' Can I call the Lamb of God, who was crucified on Calvary and who now reigns at the Father's right hand, my Beloved? Can I truly call him my Beloved? We will never consider a more important question. It would be far better for a person never to have been born than to live and die without true love for Christ (1 Cor. 16:22). Religious morality is not enough. Do I love Christ? Religious zeal and devotion is not enough. Do I love Christ? Religious works are not enough. Do I love Christ?

Love for Christ is not the ground of our salvation. Only the righteousness, and shed blood, and sovereign power of Christ can save me. Love for Christ is not the means by which we obtain salvation. Salvation comes by grace through faith. But true love for Christ is essential to salvation. Where there is no love for grace there is no grace and no salvation.

Believers are men and women who truly do love the Son of God. We do not love him as we ought. Indeed, we blush to speak of our love for him! But we do love our Redeemer. With Peter we bow our heads and say, 'Lord, thou knowest all things. Thou knowest that I love thee.' As John puts it, 'We love him because he first loved us' (1 John 4:19). His love for us precedes our love for him. His love for us causes our love for him. His love for us infinitely exceeds our love for him. But if we know him, we do love him. All who know him, trust him, worship him, and love him. There are no exceptions. Loving him, we find his word delightful, not grievous. Loving him, we find his will satisfying, not irksome. Loving him, God's people love his Word, seek his glory, delight in his salvation, and love one another (1 John 3:14; 5:1-3). Loving Christ, believers rejoice in his honour, his exaltation, and his glory. We may be reluctant to sing it in public, but believing sinners can truthfully sing to their Saviour...

> My Jesus, I love thee, I know thou art mine,
> for thee all the follies of sin I resign;
> My gracious Redeemer, my Saviour art thou,
> if ever I loved thee, my Jesus, 'tis now.

If truly we love the Lord Jesus Christ, we delight to speak of him. Love speaks of its object, defends the honour of its object, and is never ashamed of its object.

Would you grow in the love of Christ? Then seek to know the love of Christ that passes knowledge. The surest way to grow in the knowledge of his love for you and in love for him is to seek to know him. Meditate on Christ. Study Christ. Try to understand the glory of his Person. Seek to know the purity of his character. Study Christ in all his sacred offices. Think and study much about the cross, the blood, and the atonement of Christ. Meditate upon his resurrection, ascension, exaltation, and intercession. Feed your soul's hope by contemplating the Lord's glorious second coming.

Study Christ! Study Christ, so that when any ask you, 'What is thy beloved more than another beloved?', you may be ready to answer easily, quickly, and forcibly (1 John 1:1-3):

> That which was from the beginning, which we have heard, which we have seen with our eyes, which we have looked upon, and our hands have handled, of the Word of life; (For the life was manifested, and we have seen it, and bear witness, and show unto you that eternal life, which was with the Father, and was manifested unto us;) That which we have seen and heard declare we unto you, that ye also may have fellowship with us: and truly our fellowship is with the Father, and with his Son Jesus Christ.

The better we know the Lord Jesus Christ the better we will love him, speak of him, and praise him.

Christ's excellence

Throughout the Song of Solomon, and throughout the Book of God, we are given glimpses of the excellence of Christ. Here the church speaks of Christ's excellence in admiring words of deep affection — 'My beloved is white and ruddy.'

It seems to me that these words call attention to the two primary characteristics of our Lord's Person. Solomon had often seen the snow-white lambs, those emblems of purity, brought to the temple to be offered in sacrifice to the Lord. So he compares Christ to the white lamb of sacrifice. 'My beloved is white.' He had also seen the priest slit the lamb's throat, and then had seen the ruby red blood of the lamb poured out in sacrifice to God. So he puts the two together and says, 'My beloved is white and ruddy.' The white represents his immaculate purity. The red represents his sacrificial blood.

Our Lord is in himself white. He is the eternal, immaculate Son of God (1 John 1:5). Jesus Christ truly is God, the second Person of the Holy Trinity (1 John 5:7). Whiteness also represents the purity of our Saviour's life as a man (Heb. 7:25-26). Both perfect Godhood and perfect manhood are essential for him to be our Mediator and sin-atoning Substitute.

Redness refers to the sacrificial character of our Redeemer. We must never be turned aside from the great good news of the gospel and the message of substitutionary redemption. It is the foundation and the cornerstone of our faith (Rom. 1:16-17; 1 Cor. 2:1; Gal. 6:14). Christ died at Calvary as our Substitute, having all the sins of God's elect imputed to him, that all his righteousness might be justly imputed to us (2 Cor. 5:21). He was made to be sin for us by divine imputation. And we are made to be the righteousness of God in him in exactly the same way. When he had fully satisfied the righteousness and justice of God by the sacrifice of himself in the room and stead of his people, he put away our sins forever and obtained eternal redemption for us. The excellence of Christ is seen in his Person, in his work, and the fullness of grace that is ours in him (1 Cor. 1:30).

Christ's supremacy

Next, the church speaks of the supremacy of Christ. 'My beloved is white and ruddy, the chiefest among ten thousand.' These words suggest a comparison. The Lord Jesus Christ is higher, lovelier, more excellent, and greater than all others. He is the greatest Angel. He is the Messenger of the Covenant. He is the greatest Friend. He is the Friend who sticketh closer than a brother. He is the greatest Bishop. He is the Bishop of our souls. He is the greatest Shepherd. He is the good, chief, great Shepherd. He is the greatest Physician. He is the greatest Advocate (1 John 2:1-2). The angel said to Mary, 'He shall be great'; and he is great. There is none to compare unto him. Christ alone is Great!

To say that he is 'the chiefest among ten thousand' is to say that Christ is the Head, the Ruler, the Prince, the King, the Lord over all things (Ps. 2:8; Isa. 53:10-12; John 17:2; 2 Pet. 2:1; Ps.

69:18; Eph. 4:18). Christ is Head of all things (Eph. 1:22). Christ is King! He is the King of the universe, King of his church, and King in the hearts of his people.

These words might be translated, 'He is the chosen one out of ten thousand' (Ps. 89:19). He was chosen of God to be our Saviour, our Surety, our Redeemer, and our King. And he is chosen by each of his people. The marginal reference suggests that it should read, 'He is the standard bearer (ensign) among ten thousand' (Isa. 11:10). An ensign, a standard bearer, is one who holds the banner around whom the battalions rally. With a valiant heart he leads the army from victory to victory. Our Ensign is Christ himself. Our banner is the cross. Our weapon is the gospel. Our triumph is sure.

Our all-glorious Christ is flawlessly perfect in all things — in his Person — in his works — in his doctrine — in his salvation — in his dominion!

19.

Where is Christ to be found?

Song of Solomon 6:1-3

'Whither is thy beloved gone, O thou fairest among women? whither is thy beloved turned aside? that we may seek him with thee. My beloved is gone down into his garden, to the beds of spices, to feed in the gardens, and to gather lilies.) I am my beloved's, and my beloved is mine: he feedeth among the lilies.'

It is written, 'Whosoever shall call upon the name of the Lord shall be saved.' But before any sinner can or will call upon the Name of the Lord in true faith and be saved at least three things must take place.

    1. Before any man can or will trust Christ and be saved he must hear the gospel of the grace of God (Rom. 10:14-17).

    It is not enough that he hears and understands the religious opinions of men. He must hear the gospel! Martin Luther was exactly right when he said this passage of Scripture presents us with four impossibilities: (1.) It is impossible for a man to call on Christ unless he believes on Christ. (2.) It is impossible for a man to believe on Christ unless he has heard of Christ, unless he has heard the gospel of Christ. (3.) It is impossible for a man to hear of Christ without a preacher. And (4.) it is impossible for a man to preach Christ, truly to preach Christ in the power of the Holy Spirit, unless he is sent of God to do so.

No one ever has been saved and no one ever will be saved apart from hearing the gospel of the grace of God in Christ (Rom. 10:14-13; 1 Pet. 1:23-25). But what is the gospel? It is the good news of effectual atonement and accomplished redemption in Christ. The only true gospel is that gospel which answers the question — 'How can God be just and justify the ungodly?' There is but one gospel. And that gospel is the gospel of Christ's substitutionary, effectual redemption. The only way God can be both just and the Justifier of the ungodly, 'a just God and a Saviour' (Isa. 45:20), is by the substitutionary sacrifice of the Lord Jesus Christ, that sacrifice by which the Son of God fully satisfied all the claims of divine justice in the room and stead of his people.

2. Before any person can or will believe on Christ and be saved he must be regenerated by the grace and power of God the Holy Spirit (Eph. 2:1-9).

Faith, like all other graces, is the gift of God. Faith is not the cause but the result of the new birth. While we recognize that no man in the Bible is to be looked upon as having eternal life until he has faith in Christ, we also recognize that before any sinner can or will have true faith he must be given life by the sovereign power of God the Holy Spirit. Regeneration is a resurrection from the dead. It is a new creation of life. The new birth is an implanting of a new heart and a new nature. It is not the work of man, but the work of God (John 1:12-13).

3. Before anyone can or will come to Christ, calling upon him in true faith, before any man can be saved the gospel of the grace and glory of God must be revealed in his heart (2 Cor. 4:6; Matt. 16:17).

The only way any person can ever know and understand the gospel is if God himself reveals the gospel (John 3:3; 16:8-11).

In the passage now before us, the daughters of Jerusalem had heard of Christ. Though he was revealed only under the types and shadows of the Old Testament, they had heard him well described by one who knew him and loved him. They heard of the excellency of his character. They heard of the efficacy of his work. They heard of the exceeding greatness of his love.

They had heard of Christ; and that which they heard created in their hearts a desire to know Christ for themselves. So we see these daughters of Jerusalem asking where they might find the Lord. 'Whither is thy beloved gone, O thou fairest among women? Whither is thy beloved turned aside? That we may seek him with thee.' Where is Christ to be found? That is the question I want to answer in this chapter. No question could be of greater importance to eternity bound sinners. This I know — 'The Lord is good to them that wait for him, to the soul that seeketh him' (Lam. 3:25). Are you seeking him? Those who seek the Lord feel their need of him. They seek him earnestly, with all their hearts. Those who truly seek the Lord shall find him (Jer. 29:13). And those who seek the Lord must seek him in the place where he is most likely to be found. If we would know Christ and worship him, we must seek him; and it is wise to seek him in the place where he is likely to be found.

A very earnest question

Here is a very earnest question: 'Whither is thy beloved gone, O thou fairest among women? whither is thy beloved turned aside? that we may seek him with thee' (S. of S. 6:1). Here the daughters of Jerusalem, being anxious about their souls and anxious to know Christ, asked for help. They came to one who knew the Lord, and said, 'Where can we find him?' They are like those Greeks who came to Philip, and said, 'Sir, we would see Jesus.' Really, the question is this — Where can we find that Beloved One in whom sinners are accepted, justified, and forgiven? Where can we find that One who is so great and yet so gracious? Where can we find this Friend of sinners?

What inspired the daughters of Jerusalem to ask this question? They saw and recognized the blessedness of the Lord's people. They call the church of God the 'fairest among women'. They heard the faithful testimony of a believer about Christ. Though in this particular place, the Lord's church was much to be blamed, her sin and neglect were great and her heart was greatly troubled, yet she had born loving and faithful witness to Christ. It is as though she had said, 'Though I do not now enjoy his presence and a sense of communion with him, I can speak of him. I can talk of my Beloved'; and she did. She plainly declared what she had seen and heard, tasted and experienced of the Saviour's love and grace (1 John 1:1-3).

Truly, there is no better medicine for a despondent heart than to talk of Christ. There is no better cure for spiritually troubled believers than to talk of Christ. Believers may not always sense his presence, but we can always talk about him. And those who speak of him with love and faith will not be long kept from his fellowship (See vv. 4-9).

Why did the daughters of Jerusalem ask this question? We are told plainly that they wanted Christ for themselves. 'That we may seek him with thee.' Theirs was not an idle curiosity about religion. They wanted Christ. They were determined to find him. It is as though they said, 'If there is such a God and Saviour as this, we cannot rest until we find him. We must have him. Without him, we will surely perish! We are resolved, we are determined to have Christ.

> Wealth and honour we disdain, earthly comforts all are vain;
> These can never satisfy, give us Christ, or else we die!

A very confident answer

In verse 2, the Lord's redeemed gives a very confident answer to the daughters of Jerusalem: 'My beloved is gone down into his garden, to the beds of spices, to feed in the gardens, and to gather lilies.' Here the spouse, the church, the child of God was given yet another opportunity to speak of her Beloved. While she was pointing the daughters of Jerusalem to Christ, she was also ministering to her own heart. Though she had, for the time being, lost the sense of his presence by her own slothfulness, she now speaks very confidently. She says, 'I know where he is. I know where the Lord reveals himself. I know where he is to be found.' And then she shows them: 'My beloved is gone down into his garden.' Though this text speaks of Christ coming down to his garden to visit his people with grace and mercy, he has now gone up to heaven, the garden of God, where he sits upon the throne of universal dominion (Heb. 10:12).

Do any ask, 'Where is Christ to be found?' The Lord Jesus Christ is to be found in the midst of his church and people. He had said, 'I am come into my garden' (5:1). And now, the spouse seems to say, 'How foolish I have been, fretting and worrying myself about where to find him, seeking him where he is not to be found. He told me where he is. He is in his garden!' His garden is the church considered as a whole. The beds of spices and the smaller gardens may refer to the many congregations of the Lord's people. The spices and the lilies may be taken to refer to individual believers.

The church is the Lord's garden. He bought it with his blood. He encloses it with his providence. He plants it by his grace. He protects it by his power. And he dwells there. Yes, the Lord Jesus Christ dwells in the midst of his people. He is always with his beloved (Matt. 18:20; 28:20; Phil. 4:5). The Son of God still walks in the midst of the seven golden candlesticks (Rev. 1:9-20).

If you are interested in your immortal soul, if you seek the Lord, you must not neglect the public assembly of his people to worship him and hear his Word. More often than not, when the Lord intends to save one of his sheep, he causes that sheep to gather with his people in the house of worship. What is the Lord doing in his garden?

There, in the assembly of his saints, he feeds his flock by the ministry of the Word. He has chosen pastors according to his own heart, who feed his sheep with knowledge and understanding (Jer. 3:15; Acts 20:28; John 21:15-17; Eph. 4:8-16).

He also feeds himself in his garden. That is to say, he gathers the products of his own grace in his people and finds satisfaction and pleasure in the fruit of his own labour. 'The Lord taketh pleasure in those that fear him.' Matthew Henry said, 'He has many gardens, many particular churches of different sizes and shapes; but while they are his, he feeds in them all, manifests himself among them, and is well-pleased with them.'

The Lord Jesus gathers lilies in his garden, lilies with which he is pleased to entertain and adorn himself. Of course, these lilies are his own people, the flowers of his grace and mercy. There was a great gathering of his lilies, his elect people, by his death upon the cross (Eph. 2:4-6; John 11:51-52). Today, by the grace and power of the Holy Spirit, through the ministry of the gospel, Christ is still gathering his lilies. He gathers his lilies from his garden when he calls them up to glory. Soon he is coming to gather all of his lilies (1 Thess. 4:13-18). One of the old writers said, 'He picks the lilies one by one, and gathers them to himself. And there will be a general harvest of them in the great day, when he will send forth his angels, to gather all his lilies, that he may be forever glorified and admired in them.'

A very comforting assurance

In verse 3, the church, the bride of Christ speaks a word of very comforting assurance to her own heart: 'I am my beloved's, and my beloved is mine: he feedeth among the lilies.' Though the Lord has withdrawn from her the sense and manifestation of his presence, she was comforted by faith in his Word. She was assured of her relationship with him, because she knew it depended not upon her faithfulness but his faithfulness. She says, 'I am my beloved's; and my beloved is mine: he feedeth among the lilies.' In spite of her own sin, negligence, and unbelief, she expresses three things about which she was sure. From these she draws great comfort.

First, she says, 'I am my beloved's.' She had acted shamefully toward him. Therefore, in love he chastened her for a while. But she knew that her standing was not upon her works, but upon his works. Her acceptance was not by works, but by grace. Therefore, she takes a fresh hold upon that firm and everlasting covenant, which stands unbroken in spite of our many sins (Ps. 89:30-35).

She says, 'I am,' even now, 'my beloved's.' Let every believer look upon Christ with such confident faith, knowing our own sin and corruption, and declare, 'I am my beloved's by an eternal gift, by a loving election, by a special redemption, and by a distinguishing grace. Yes, I am his! Nothing that I have done or ever shall do can change that fact.' What comfort there is in such an assurance!

Second, she declares, 'my beloved is mine!' This is even better. Since Christ is mine, I neither want nor need anything else. He is all I need. Here is the glory and beauty of faith. It believes Christ, even when he is not seen and his presence is not felt. Child of God, your salvation depends not upon feeling or experience, but upon Christ! He is yours, because the Father gave him to you. He is yours, because he swore that he would be. He said, 'I will be for thee.' He is yours, because he revealed himself to you. He is yours, because you trust him, because he gives you faith to trust him.

Third, she says, 'He feedeth among the lilies.' She seems to be saying, 'I know that Christ is mine and that I am his. And I know that he feeds among the lilies. He meets with his people in his garden, talks with them, and communes with them, and reveals himself to them. Therefore, I know if I am in his garden when he comes among his lilies, I will meet with him again.'

Let us ever rest confidently upon our great Saviour's covenant faithfulness (2 Sam. 23:5). And let us ever cherish the privilege of gathering with his saints in his garden, where he still 'feedeth among the lilies' (Heb. 10:25).

20.

Five pictures of the church

Song of Solomon 6:4-10

'Thou art beautiful, O my love, as Tirzah, comely as Jerusalem, terrible as an army with banners. Turn away thine eyes from me, for they have overcome me: thy hair is as a flock of goats that appear from Gilead. Thy teeth are as a flock of sheep which go up from the washing, whereof every one beareth twins, and there is not one barren among them.) As a piece of a pomegranate are thy temples within thy locks. There are threescore queens, and fourscore concubines, and virgins without number. My dove, my undefiled is but one; she is the only one of her mother, she is the choice one of her that bare her. The daughters saw her, and blessed her; yea, the queens and the concubines, and they praised her. Who is she that looketh forth as the morning, fair as the moon, clear as the sun, and terrible as an army with banners?'

In these verses our Lord Jesus describes his church as he sees it, and as it truly is. When I use this term, 'the church', I mean the people of God, not a physical building, not a religious denomination, not even a local assembly, but the whole company of God's elect, in heaven and in earth, all who have been saved, are saved, and shall yet be saved by the grace of God.

Using this term, 'the church', in this way, I am using it in the way Paul did when he said, 'Christ loved the church and gave himself for it' (Eph. 5:25). It is the church universal which Paul speaks of when he says that Christ has been made 'the head over all things to the church' (Eph. 1:22). This is 'the church of God which he hath purchased with his own blood' (Acts 20:28). It is the church universal our Lord Jesus Christ spoke of when he said, 'Upon this rock I will build my church; and the gates of hell shall not prevail against it' (Matt. 16:18).

I stress this because many fail to understand that God's church is one, that the body and bride of Christ is one, and that our Lord's one body and church is made up of all his elect. All of God's true people, considered as one, make up the church, the universal body and bride of Christ. All of God's elect, all true believers of every age and every place make up the church of Christ.

> Elect from every nation,
> Yet one o'er all the earth:
> Her charter of salvation,
> One Lord, one faith, one birth.

The church did not begin with Paul, it did not begin with Peter, and it did not begin with John the Baptist. The church did not begin at Pentecost, or at Calvary. The church of our Lord Jesus Christ began with Adam. The earliest worshippers in the church of our Lord were Adam and Eve, and their Son, Abel. And the church of Christ will be complete when the last of God's elect has been regenerated and united to Christ by faith. When the last sheep has been brought into the fold, the fold will be complete, and the Shepherd will be satisfied.

See that you understand what I am saying. The church is the body and bride of Christ; and all who are in Christ are in the church. All who were chosen in Christ are in the church. All who were redeemed in Christ are in the church. All who were justified in Christ are in the church. All who are regenerated in Christ are in the church. All who are preserved in Christ are in the church. All who shall be raised with Christ are in the church. If you and I are in Christ we are in that church which is his body. If we are saved by the grace of God we are members of the Lord's church; and we are members in good standing.

Our heavenly Bridegroom, the Lord Jesus Christ gives us five pictures of the church. He describes the church as he sees it. He tells us what his church truly is. And what our Lord here says of the church collectively is true of all believers individually.

Because of her sinful neglect, the Lord had temporarily withdrawn from his church the sense of his manifest presence (5:2-6). Though she did not have the comforting sense of his presence, she cherished him in her heart and held him by faith (5:9-6:3). She was in great sorrow, because of the Lord's absence. But she never ceased to love him. And she never ceased to believe him. She rested her soul upon Christ alone, not upon her own feelings and experiences (6:3). Being confident of his love, mercy, grace, and faithfulness, she sings, even in her low condition, 'I am my beloved's, and my beloved is mine: he feedeth among the lilies.' In this passage, our Lord graciously reveals himself again to his church to comfort and assure her again of his mercy, love, and grace. Here he graciously assures us of his love for us, and our acceptance with him by giving us five pictures of his church as he sees us.

An army

First, the church of Christ is an army in this world. 'Thou art beautiful, O my love, as Tirzah, comely as Jerusalem, terrible as an army with banners' (v. 4).

'Tirzah' was a city in the tribe of Manasseh. It means 'pleasant and acceptable'. 'Jerusalem' is the city of God. It is symbolically a type of the church (Gal. 4:26; Heb. 12:22). Believers in this world are soldiers enlisted in an army (Eph. 6:10-20). We are soldiers in the territory of a hostile enemy. Our banner is the glorious gospel of Christ, Christ crucified, Christ himself (Isa. 11:12).

Christ, our Mighty Captain, has given us our marching orders (Matt. 28:18-20). It is our responsibility to march against the very gates of hell, conquering the world for our King by the gospel. It is our responsibility to stand firm in defence of the gospel. Our triumph and ultimate victory is sure (Matt. 16:18).

Object of love

Second, the church is the object of Christ's love. 'Turn away thine eyes from me, for they have overcome me: thy hair is as a flock of goats that appear from Gilead' (v. 5).

Here our Lord assures his troubled and afflicted people that they are the objects of his love. His love toward us has not changed. Though he does, at times, withdraw from us his manifest presence, he never ceases to love us (Isa. 54:7-10). The love of God for his people is without cause, without beginning, without change, and without end.

Every human tie may perish;
Friend to friend unfaithful prove;
Mothers cease their own to cherish;
Heaven and earth at last remove;
But no changes attend Jehovah's love.

Zion's Friend in nothing alters,
Though all others may and do;
His is love that never falters,
Always to its object true.
Happy Zion! Crowned with mercies ever new.

Here is a strange expression of love — 'Turn away thine eyes from me, for they have overcome me.' Our Saviour uses the expressions of a passionate lover to express the tenderness of a compassionate Redeemer. With these words, our Saviour seems to say, I cannot resist those eyes that look to me. I will forgive and forget all that is past. The Lord of Glory is overcome by his people when they look unto him!

We look to him with sorrowful eyes in repentance. We look to him with hopeful eyes in faith. We look to him with sincere eyes in love. And he is overcome! He cannot resist the look of faith! Child of God, even when the Lord hides his face keep on looking to him. The eyes of repentance, love, and faith will soon prevail. He so loves us that he is willing to be overcome by us!

Perfect

Third, the church is perfect in the eyes of Christ. 'Thy teeth are as a flock of sheep which go up from the washing, whereof every one beareth twins, and there is not one barren among them. As a piece of a pomegranate are thy temples within thy locks' (vv. 6-7).

Here our Lord repeats almost word for word the description he had given of his bride's beauty and perfection earlier (4:1-3), before the sad decline described in chapter five. He is saying, 'Nothing has changed between us.' What grace! We are accepted in the Beloved. Our shameful sin, ingratitude, coldness of heart, unfaithfulness, and unbelief will never cause us to be any the less accepted. All our beauty, all our perfection, all our holiness is in him. Nothing can change that. In Christ we are redeemed. In Christ we are righteous. In Christ we are accepted — always accepted — unconditionally accepted. In Christ we are forgiven. The forgiveness of sin in Christ is free, full, final, and forever! The Lord will never impute sin to his people (Ps. 32:1-2; Rom. 4:8). We are forgiven!

One body

Fourth, the church is one body in Christ. 'There are threescore queens, and fourscore concubines, and virgins without number. My dove, my undefiled is but one; she is the only one of her mother, she is the choice one of her that bare her. The daughters saw her, and blessed her; yea, the queens and the concubines, and they praised her' (vv. 8-9)

Other kings have queens, their wives and concubines, and mistresses, and virgins, and maidens. But Christ our King makes all of his people one. In the kingdom of grace there is no such thing as rank, and class, and position. The people of God are one (Col. 3:11; 1 Cor. 12:12-27). We all have the same Father. We all have the same Elder Brother. We all have the same indwelling Spirit. We all have the same eternal inheritance. Let us, therefore, live as one body in Christ (Eph. 4:1-6). Let us strive together as one body to glorify the Lord our God.

The light of the world

Fifth, the church of Christ is the light of the world. 'Who is she that looketh forth as the morning, fair as the moon, clear as the sun, and terrible as an army with banners?' (v. 10).

The church of God shines as the light of the sun in this world, giving forth light to them that sit in darkness (Matt. 5:14). In its beginning the church was like the rising of the morning sun, the dawning of light. At its best in this world, the church is like the moon at night, reflecting the light of the Sun of Righteousness. When we are complete in the kingdom of glory, we shall shine forth as the sun (Matt. 13:43). In that day, we shall be clothed with the Sun, with Christ the Sun of Righteousness, and like him we shall display the eternal glory of God (Rev. 12:1; Isa. 30:26).

All of these pictures were given that we might rest in his love. Why shouldn't we? He does.

> The LORD hath taken away thy judgements, he hath cast out thine enemy: the king of Israel, even the LORD, is in the midst of thee: thou shalt not see evil any more. In that day it shall be said to Jerusalem, Fear thou not: and to Zion, Let not thine hands be slack. The LORD thy God in the midst of thee is mighty; he will save, he will rejoice over thee with joy; he will rest in his love, he will joy over thee with singing (Zeph. 3:15-17).

21.

Inward conflicts

Song of Solomon 6:11-13

'I went down into the garden of nuts to see the fruits of the valley, and to see whether the vine flourished, and the pomegranates budded. Or ever I was aware, my soul made me like the chariots of Amminadib. Return, return, O Shulamite; return, return, that we may look upon thee. What will ye see in the Shulamite? As it were the company of two armies.'

In these verses our Lord speaks to his church, not in her time of doubt and despair while she was seeking him, but he speaks here to his church in her very best condition. She had just begun to again enjoy his blessed fellowship. Christ has now returned to his spouse. The breach she had made by her neglect, he had healed by his grace. There was now a sweet renewing of love and fellowship.

Christ speaks

In verse 11 our Lord speaks to his beloved church and says:

Though I had withdrawn myself from you and gave you no comfort for a while, even then I had my eye upon you, even then I was watching over my garden with tenderness, love, and care. Though you did not see me, I saw you. I will never forsake the apple of my eye or the work of my hands.

In verse 12, our Saviour tells us how that he was overcome by our broken, aching hearts and how anxiously he returned to his people who cried after him. It is as though he said, 'I could hide my face no longer. My love for you compelled me, with irresistible force, to return to you. Almost before I knew it, my soul set me on the chariots of my willing people' (Marginal translation).

Joseph hid himself from his brethren, because of their evil actions, to chastise them. But he could no longer refrain himself. His loving heart broken, he burst into tears, and said, 'I am Joseph' (Gen. 45:1, 3). So our Saviour cannot and will not forever hide his face from the objects of his love (Isa. 54:7-10).

We ought to be a willing people, seeking Christ always in love, faith, and hope. These will be like chariots to bring him to us. If we continue seeking the Lord, he will return to us in due time. 'No chariots sent for Christ shall return empty' (Matthew Henry). Our Lord will return to us, because of his own grace, love, mercy, and faithfulness. We can do nothing to win his favour. He is gracious, because he will be gracious. He loves us, because he will love us. He returns to us, because he will return to us. He is faithful!

In verse 13, the Lord Jesus, having returned to his beloved church, courts her, wooing her heart, and invites her to return to him. 'Return, return, O Shulamite; return, return, that we may look upon thee.' Solomon chose his bride and espoused her to himself, giving her his name. 'Shulamite' should be translated 'Solyma'. The Hebrew word is the feminine of the name 'Solomon'. The Lord Jesus Christ has made us so thoroughly one with himself that he has given us his Name. He is our Solomon, and we are his Solyma (Compare Jeremiah 23:6 and 33:16). All that our Lord Jesus Christ is, he has made us to be by divine imputation.

This name 'Shulamite' or 'Solyma' means 'perfection'. Believers are perfect in Christ. We are complete in him. Being washed in his blood, we are spotless. Being robed in his righteousness, we are glorious, holy, and pure.

This name 'Shulamite' or 'Solyma' also means 'peace'. 'Therefore, being justified, by faith we have peace with God through Jesus Christ our Lord.' We are no longer at enmity with God. Our consciences no longer accuse us. Peace has been made for us with God. The warfare is ended. God's sword has been sheathed in our Saviour's heart. Justice no longer cries against us, but for us.

Our Lord graciously calls for us to return unto him. Four times he says, 'Return, return, O Solyma, return, return.' How willing our all-glorious Christ is to have us in his fellowship and communion! He says, 'Return to me.' Return to your first simple faith. Return to your first tender love. Return to the place where we first met, the cross.

Now catch the Master's next loving words. Our Lord says to his beloved, he says to you and me, 'Return, return, that we may look upon thee.' He seems to say, 'You have not been with me much alone lately. You have neglected reading my Word and hearing it. I have seldom heard your voice, or seen your face. Return, return unto me, that we (God the Father, God the Son, and God the Holy Spirit) may look upon you. If you return, we will look upon you again. I will show you my face again. We will look upon you in love. We will look upon you in forgiveness. We will look upon you in kindness. We will look upon you in pleasantness and satisfaction.'

The bride speaks

But then, in the second part of verse 13, we hear the bride, the church, the people of God speaking. Being convinced of her own sin, being full of shame, she confesses her frustration with herself. She thinks that there is no beauty in her, nothing in her that he could want to see. 'What will ye see in Solyma? As it were the company of two armies.' She is saying, 'There is nothing in me but conflict and confusion. In my heart two armies are at war. If you look upon me, you will see a raging battle, good fighting evil, light contending with darkness. I am not worth looking upon. I am a house divided against itself.'

This is a true and accurate description of the people of God. All of God's elect experience constant warfare within, constant conflict between the flesh and the Spirit, so long as we live in this body of flesh. This conflict, this warfare causes us so much pain and trouble.

A painful fact

These inward conflicts are facts in every believer's life. The believer's life is not all sweets. It is not all joy and peace. Faith in Christ will bring some bitter conflicts, which will cause God's child much pain, much toil, and many tears. The struggles between the flesh and the Spirit are evident enough to all who are born of God. To the unbelieving, unregenerate religionist, true Christians are confusing paradoxes. We are the happiest and the most mournful people in the world. We are the richest and the poorest people on earth. We are men and women who possess perfect peace, yet we are always at war.

We have seen traces of this conflict throughout the Song of Solomon (1:5; 3:1; 5:2). We see these inward conflicts throughout the Psalms of David (Ps. 42; 43; 73). We see them dealt with and explained in the writings of the Apostle Paul (Rom. 7:14-25; Gal. 5:16-18). And we see these terrible inward conflicts in our own daily experience of grace.

The people of God throughout the centuries have had the same struggles that we now have. John Bunyan wrote a book about his conflicts of heart and soul, which he titled, The Holy War. Richard Sibbes wrote a similar book called, The Soul's Conflict. Though we are born of God, God's saints in this world have a corrupt nature within, which would drive us to sin. Yet, we have within us a righteous nature, which would draw us into perfect conformity and union with Christ. Between these two forces of good and evil there is no peace (1 John 3:7-9).

Two natures

This conflict is caused by and begins in regeneration. C. H. Spurgeon said, 'The reigning power of sin falls dead the moment a man is converted, but the struggling power of sin does not die until the man dies.' A new nature has been planted within us; but the old nature is not eradicated.

Do not think for a moment that the old nature dies in regeneration, or even that it gets better. Flesh is flesh, and will never be anything but flesh. Noah, Lot, Moses, David, and Peter, like all other believers, had to struggle with this fact. We need no proof of the fact that God's people in this world have two warring natures within beyond an honest examination of our own hearts and lives. Our best thoughts are corrupted with sin. Our most fervent prayers are defiled by lusts of the flesh. Our reading of Holy Scripture is corrupted by carnal passions. Our most spiritual worship is marred by the blackness within. Our most holy aspirations are vile. Our purest love for our Saviour is so corrupted by our love of self and love for this world that we can hardly call our love for Christ love. From time to time we have all found by bitter experience the truthfulness of the hymn...

Prone to wander, Lord, I feel it!
Prone to leave the God I love:
Here's my heart, O take and seal it,
Seal it for Thy courts above.

Without question, our heavenly Father could remove all this evil from us, but he chooses not to. Why?

Good effect

The fact is, these inward conflicts do have some good effect. Hard as they are to bear now, in heaven's glory we will look back upon these days of great evil with gratitude, and see the wisdom and goodness of God in all of our struggles with sin. Our struggles with sin help humble us and curb our pride. Our struggles with sin force us to lean upon Christ alone for all our salvation (1 Cor. 1:30), and confess with Jonah, 'Salvation is of the Lord.' Struggling hard with sin, we find that 'Christ is all' indeed. Our struggles with sin cause us to prize the faithfulness of our God (Lam. 3:1-27). Our struggles with sin upon this earth will make the glorious victory of heaven sweeter. And our struggles with sin make us rejoice in the fact that 'salvation is of the Lord'.

I do not doubt that in eternity we will be made to see that God wisely and graciously allowed us to fall into one evil to keep us from a greater evil, or to make us more useful in his hands. Certainly, an honest acknowledgement of the sin that is in us, and of the fact that we are never without sin (1 John 1:8-10) ought to make us gracious, kind, forgiving, and patient with one another.

Soon over

Blessed be God, these inward conflicts will soon be over (Phil. 1:6; Jude 24-25). We shall soon drop this earthly tabernacle and shall be completely free from sin. We shall be perfect, personally perfect, at last. We shall be triumphant in the end. In that day when our God shall make all things new, the former things shall not only pass away, they shall be remembered no more! All the evil consequences of sin shall be forever removed. We shall be forever 'faultless before the presence of his glory with exceeding joy'.

Yet, so long as we live in this world we will be 'as the company of two armies'. So I give you this word of admonition — 'Keep thy heart with all diligence: for out of it are the issues of life' (Prov. 4:23). Keep your heart tender. Keep your heart in the fellowship of

Christ. Keep you heart full of the Word. Keep your heart in prayer. Keep your heart full of the cross. Keep your heart full of Christ and rest your soul upon Christ.

22.

Tender words of intimate love

Song of Solomon 7:1-13

'How beautiful are thy feet with shoes, O prince's daughter! the joints of thy thighs are like jewels, the work of the hands of a cunning workman. Thy navel is like a round goblet, which wanteth not liquor: thy belly is like an heap of wheat set about with lilies. Thy two breasts are like two young roes that are twins. Thy neck is as a tower of ivory; thine eyes like the fishpools in Heshbon, by the gate of Bathrabbim: thy nose is as the tower of Lebanon which looketh toward Damascus. Thine head upon thee is like Carmel, and the hair of thine head like purple; the king is held in the galleries. How fair and how pleasant art thou, O love, for delights! This thy stature is like to a palm tree, and thy breasts to clusters of grapes. I said, I will go up to the palm tree, I will take hold of the boughs thereof: now also thy breasts shall be as clusters of the vine, and the smell of thy nose like apples; And the roof of thy mouth like the best wine for my beloved, that goeth down sweetly, causing the lips of those that are asleep to speak. I am my beloved's, and his desire is toward me. Come, my beloved, let us go forth into the field; let us lodge in the villages. Let us get up early to the vineyards; let us see if the vine flourish, whether the tender grape appear, and the pomegranates bud forth: there will I give thee my loves. The mandrakes give a smell, and at our gates are all manner of pleasant fruits, new and old, which I have laid up for thee, O my beloved.'

In this seventh chapter of the Song of Solomon the Lord Jesus Christ gives us a very tender, intimate, and loving description of his love and esteem for his bride, the church. He tells us, in the most intimate terms, that he both loves us and takes delight in us (vv. 1-9). Then, in verses 10-13, the bride, the church, expresses her love for Christ. She tells him how that she loves him, delights in him, and greatly desires to be in communion and fellowship with him.

The intimate language of this chapter to carnal and self-righteous men will probably be both confusing and offensive. But, to those who know the love of Christ and whose hearts are truly in love with the Son of God, this seventh chapter of The Song of Loves is both delightful and precious. Commenting on this passage, Matthew Henry said, 'Such mutual esteem and endearment there is between Christ and believers. And what is heaven but an everlasting interchanging of loves between the holy God and holy souls!'

Husbands and wives

These expressions of love are between Christ and his church. They must be understood allegorically, in a spiritual sense. Yet, we have here a pattern and example of that love and tenderness which should characterize every home. The Holy Spirit here gives us a pattern of love for husbands and wives. In Ephesians 5:22-32, the apostle Paul makes it very clear that the relationship of a husband and wife, if it is what it should be, is a picture of the relationship between Christ and his church. Believing men and women ought to work at making their homes palaces of love and happiness for the glory of Christ.

Marriage was ordained and established by God for the propagation of the race and for the happiness of man (Gen. 2:18). Our Lord Jesus Christ showed his approval for marriage when he attended the wedding in Cana and provided wine for the guests. By his presence, our Lord honoured and sanctified the marriage (John 2). Marriage is honourable for all men (Heb. 13:4). We must not look upon marriage as a carnal thing. And we should not look upon the conjugal privileges of husbands and wives as something evil or distasteful. Paul says that 'marriage is honourable in all, and the bed undefiled'. Men and women need to get over their silly, prudish ideas about marriage (1 Cor. 7:1-5).

The relationship of a husband and wife should be a picture of the relationship of Christ and his church. They are no longer two, but one. They are to live together in mutual, self-sacrificing love. The husband is to love, protect, and provide for his wife. The wife is to love, reverence, submit to, and obey her husband.

Christ and his church

Here, in the Song of Solomon, chapter 7, we have tender words of intimate love between Christ and his church; and they give us a picture of that love which should characterize the husband-wife relationship. We will go through this chapter giving very briefly its interpretation, showing the love and esteem Christ has for his church and the love and esteem believers have for Christ. Then I will draw some applications, which I hope will be helpful for us as husbands and wives. We should seek to follow our Lord and seek his glory in our homes.

Christ speaks

In verses 1-9, we hear the Lord Jesus Christ speaking to his church in tender, loving, thoughtful, and endearing terms. Notice the title the Son of God gives to his church — 'O Prince's Daughter'. The Lord himself is 'the Prince of the kings of the earth'. He is 'the Prince of Glory' and 'the Prince of Peace'. He calls us his daughter. We are the Prince's daughter by birth. We are born from above, begotten of God. We are his workmanship. We bear the image of the King of kings. We are the Prince's daughter by marriage. Christ, the Son of God, has betrothed us to himself, making us the Prince's daughter, the very children of God. As the Prince's daughter, we have been made heirs of the Prince of the kings of the earth.

Our Lord here describes the beauty of his church in his own eyes (vv. 1-5). In our own eyes we see that there is nothing beautiful in us. Our souls are like the company of two warring armies. We are humbled with a sense of our sin, our shame, and our worthlessness. We are not worthy of such love as his.

But Christ himself here speaks to us, sinful though we are, to express his love, assuring us that he loves us and delights in us. These tender, loving words are thoughtful and endearing. The church had defiled herself. She needed to be assured of his love. So our thoughtful Redeemer assures us that his love has not changed. In Christ we are perfect, and he declares that we are. The Lord looks his bride over from head to foot, and describes her as having a tenfold beauty in his eyes, a beauty which no one else could have in his eyes.

1. 'How beautiful are thy feet with shoes.' He has set our feet free and adorned them with the gospel of peace to walk in liberty.

2. 'The joints of thy thighs are like jewels.' The principles that strengthen us and determine how we walk through this world, like the knee and hip joints, are as jewels in his sight. They are principles of faith and love toward him for the glory of God. They are produced in us by God the Holy Spirit, as 'the work of the hands of a cunning workman' (Eph. 2:10).

3. 'Thy navel is like a round goblet.' Perhaps, as some suggest, the reference here is not to the 'navel' itself, but to a jewel worn to cover it, that it refers to 'the clothing of wrought gold' (Ps 45:13), representing the beautiful robe of Christ's righteousness with which his church is adorned. Perhaps the word refers to the navel itself, symbolizing the fulness of life that is ours in Christ. It is compared to a cup full of wine, refreshing and invigorating. It is well shaped and full of life, not uncut, bleeding, and loathsome, like it was when he found us (Ezek. 16:4). The fear of the Lord is said to be 'health to the navel' (Prov. 3:8).

4. 'Thy belly is like a heap of wheat, set about with lilies.' The

wheat refers to fruitfulness (Gal. 5:22-23). The flowers refer to beauty and pleasantness.

5. 'Thy two breasts are like two young roes that are twins.' This refers to the Word of God, the Old and New Testaments, like twins, they are in perfect agreement, showing forth the riches, the glory, and the grace of Christ (1 Pet. 2:2).

6. 'Thy neck is a tower of ivory.' The faith of God's elect, by which we are joined to Christ our Head, is both strong and precious.

7. 'Thine eyes like the fish pools in Heshbon, by the gate of Bathrabbim.' Eyes of repentance and faith, of love and devotion, of sincerity and truth. The eyes that weep over sin are as beautiful fountains in the eyes of Christ.

8. 'Thy nose is as the tower of Lebanon which looketh toward Damascus.' This speaks of the boldness and courage of the church in facing her enemies and in the cause of Christ.

9. 'Thine head upon thee is like Carmel, and the hair of thine head like purple.' Christ our Head is exalted above the earth and reigns as King over all the earth.

10. A woman's beauty is in her head, and the hair of her head is her glory. Even so, Christ our Head is our great Glory and Beauty. Our glory is altogether in Christ's blood atonement and royal exaltation as our Saviour. The church's hair 'may be said to be like "purple" because of their royal dignity, being made kings unto God by Christ, and because of their being washed in the purple blood of Christ' (John Gill). We have no beauty except what we have in and from him. And his greatest beauty is seen in his agony at the cross, when his hair was dyed crimson and purple.

In verses 5-9, our Lord tells us of the complacency, satisfaction, and delight he has in his church. 'The king is held in the galleries' (v. 5). Imagine that! The Lord Jesus Christ, the Son of God, the God of Glory is so ravished by the beauty of his church, the beauty he has bestowed upon and wrought in her, that he is held at a stand by the sight of her! The Lord Jesus Christ has so adorned us and made us so beautiful in his sight that he delights in us (Ezek. 16:13-14). Our great Saviour delights in the beauty of his people, his righteousness (vv. 6-7). The Lord of Glory delights in the company of his people (v. 8). Christ Jesus, our great God, delights in the prayers and praises of his people (v. 9).

The church speaks

In verses 10-13, we see that the church, all believing hearts, is overcome by the love of Christ. The love of Christ, once it is revealed and known, is an irresistible love. Does Christ so love me? Then, surely I shall love him (1 John 4:19). In these verses, the church, the bride, acknowledges five things that I hope as you read them you, too, can honestly acknowledge.

First, she acknowledges that she belongs to Christ (v. 10) — 'I am my beloved's.' We belong to him by his own eternal choice of us in electing love (John 15:16). We are his by special purchase (Eph. 5:25-27). We belong to our Saviour by the commit of personal faith because we freely give ourselves to him (Mark 8:35). And we belong to the Son of God by the consecration of love to him (1 John 4:19).

Second, she expresses, to his praise and glory, that she is confident of his love for her — 'his desire is toward me!' He desires our salvation so much that it was the joy set before him, for which he endured the cross. His heart's desire is that we may be with him where he is and that we may know the love wherewith he has loved us (John 17:23-24).

Third, she acknowledges a desire to be with him, in his company, and in his fellowship (v. 11) — 'Come, my beloved, let us go forth into the field; let us lodge in the villages.'

Thou, O Christ, art all I want,
More than all in thee I find.

Fourth, she acknowledges a desire to know the true condition of her own soul (v. 12) — 'Let us get up early to the vineyards; let us see if the vine flourish, whether the tender grape appear, and the pomegranates bud forth.'

Fifth, she acknowledges her love and devotion for Christ (vv. 12-13) — 'There will I give thee my loves. The mandrakes give a smell, and at our gates are all manner of pleasant fruits, new and old, which I have laid up for thee, O my beloved.' She promises him her love. She promises him herself. All that she is and all that she has she holds in love for him and gives to him.

Lessons

There are lessons here for both husbands and wives. Love needs no law. It is a law unto itself. Love needs no motive. It is a motive unto itself. If you love your wife, you want to please her and do her good. You need no commandment in that regard. If you love your husband, you want to please him and honour him. Love needs no law or motivation beyond itself. But even love needs instruction. And here our Lord gives us some instructions in love, by way of his own example.

By his example, our Lord gives husbands some clear instructions about loving their wives. Let every believing husband imitate the Son of God in faithfulness to, thoughtfulness of, and giving honour to his wife. Happy is that woman whose husband seeks to imitate the Lord Jesus in intimate tenderness, affection, and devotion (Eph. 5:32).

The spouse here stands as an example of the love women should show to their husbands. Let every believing wife reverence her husband (v. 10), find satisfaction with and in her husband (v. 11), and submit to her husband (v. 12). Happy is that man whose wife gives herself and her love to him (v. 12), and desires to please him (v. 13).

Let us safely rest in our Saviour's love. Lets us keep our hearts in the love of Christ. Let us imitate the love of Christ in our homes.

23.

'Let him kiss me'

Song of Solomon 1:2

'Let him kiss me with the kisses of his mouth: for thy love is better than wine.'

After reviewing our Saviour's words of tender, intimate love and affection for us (7:1-13), does your heart not again cry, 'Let him kiss me'? A kiss is one of the most tender expressions of affection and love known to man. It is universally understood. The very first thing a mother does with a newborn baby as she holds it to her breast is kiss it. The very last thing we do with a dying loved one is plant a farewell kiss on the face we shall never again see in this world. Here is a bride longing to be kissed, and kissed, and kissed by her beloved. The bride is the church of God. Her Beloved is the Lord Jesus Christ, the King of Glory. What a great, noble, ennobling, burning desire this is. 'Let him kiss me with the kisses of his mouth: for thy love is better than wine.'

   This is an enormous desire. It is a privilege, beyond comparison, to have the Lord Jesus Christ himself kiss us. In days of old, it was considered a high, high honour for a king to stretch out his hand and allow one of his subjects to kiss just his hand. Here, the

Shulamite expresses a desire that would be utterly unthinkable. She desired the king himself to kiss her, not only to kiss her, but to kiss her intimately, passionately, and repeatedly with the kisses of his mouth! She desired all the kisses he had to offer.

The desire would be unthinkable, except for one thing — she knew. She was fully convinced that the king wanted to kiss her as much as she wanted to be kissed by him! But there is much more here than a story of romance between a Shulamite woman and King Solomon. This is an expression of a soul in love with the Lord Jesus Christ, longing for him to come in sweet manifestations of himself and his love, with the kisses of his mouth.

The request

Meditate on this heartfelt request. 'Let him kiss me with the kisses of his mouth.' Really, the text might be read, 'O that he would kiss me with the kisses of his mouth!' She speaks as one who has experienced Christ's love, as one who knew how sweet the kisses of his mouth are. She had tasted that the Lord is gracious. She had found grace in his lips, overflowing, abundant and sweet. She is, therefore, anxious and ardent in her request, venting her soul passionately before him.

Though she does not call him by name, clearly, this is a request addressed to Christ himself, though spoken publicly before others. As John Gill put it, 'She had him so much in her thoughts, her love was so fixed on him, she knew him so well, and had had so much converse with him, that she thought there was no need to mention his name; but that every one must very well know who she designed.' She speaks of him as if there were no one else in the world but him. Indeed, there is none other but him for our soul: 'Whom have I in heaven but thee? and there is none upon earth that I desire besides thee' (Ps. 73:25).

The kisses

What are these kisses? How can the Lord Jesus kiss us? Obviously, the kisses with which the Son of God kisses his people, the kisses by which he manifestly expresses his love to us, by which he assures us of his everlasting love for us, are the manifestations of himself to us.

One of the most instructive and most delightful pictures of God's great grace is that which is drawn by Luke's pen of the prodigal son (Luke 15). The only time in the Bible that God Almighty is portrayed as being in a hurry is there. When his son was yet a great way off, the father saw him, jumped off his throne, ran to meet him, fell on his neck, and kissed him, and kissed him, and kissed him, and kissed him! What a great picture that is of our God welcoming poor sinners into his kingdom!

Here, however, is one who has experienced that grace and love, one whose soul is wed to the Son of God, crying, 'Let him kiss me with the kisses of his mouth.' These kisses are fresh manifestations and discoveries of our Saviour's love to us, by some precious word of promise from his mouth applied to us by his Spirit. As in the picture of the prodigal's reception, we owe our salvation to the kisses of our Saviour. In regeneration, the Son of God kissed us with his grace and openly wed himself to us forever. He betrothed us unto him in righteousness, in judgement, in loving kindness, in tender mercies, and even in faithfulness, and caused us to know him (Hos. 2:19-20).

He kissed us with the kiss of redemption, that great act of his love in which mercy and truth met together and righteousness and peace kissed each other (Ps. 85:10). He bought us to himself (Hos. 2:3; Tit. 2:14), distinctly and particularly bought us. When he called us by his grace, he declared, 'I have redeemed thee, I have called thee by thy name, and thou art mine' (Isa. 43:1).

With that came the kiss of reconciliation, by which our Saviour wrapped us in his arms of mercy and declared in our very hearts that our sins are all put away and that we have been made the very righteousness of God in him, reconciled to God by his blood and reconciled to God by the power of his grace (Rom. 8:1-4).

Not only has our Saviour kissed us, he commands us to kiss him (Ps. 2:11-12), which is to put our trust in him. When he kisses us in grace, we kiss him in faith. The sinner loved, chosen, redeemed and called by the grace of God is kissed by Christ and is sweetly compelled by irresistible grace to kiss him. He espouses us; and we espouse him. He chooses us for his bride; and we choose him for our husband. He loves us; and 'we love him because he first loved us' (1 John 4:19).

The reason

'Let him kiss me with the kisses of his mouth.' That is our desire. Here is the reason for it. We have discovered that 'for thy love is better than wine'. The love of Christ, that love with which he loves us, that love which in its length is longer than eternity, in its breadth is broader than the earth, in its depth reaches the lowest of sinners, and in its height ascends to the very throne of God is better than wine.

Wine is a temporary cordial for the body's weakness. Christ's love is the everlasting cordial for our immortal souls! Wine may relieve worldly sorrows for a brief moment. Christ's love will cure all sorrows forever! Wine, if used too freely, will only add drunkenness to thirst. Christ's love is such that those who drink the deepest draughts, those who are most intoxicated by it are most blessed and never injured. The love of Christ is more than pleasant. It is always effectual. It raises sinners dead in trespasses and sins to eternal life. It raises us from the dunghill to the King's chamber. It delivers us from all curse and condemnation. It makes us the sons of God. It infallibly saves us from the second death. It brings us to eternal glory.

Look yonder to Calvary's cursed tree. Behold our crucified Substitute, and behold how he loved us! Oh, let our souls be ravished with his love! Have we tasted the love of Christ? Have we drunk this sweet wine? If so, we are constrained to cry out, 'Stay me with flagons, for I am sick of love!' (Song 2:5). Let this now be the prayer of our hearts — 'Let him kiss me with the kisses of his mouth; for thy love is better than wine!'

24.

'Come, my beloved'

Song of Solomon 7:10-13

'I am my beloved's, and his desire is toward me. Come, my be-loved, let us go forth into the field; let us lodge in the villages. Let us get up early to the vineyards; let us see if the vine flourish, whether the tender grape appear, and the pomegranates bud forth: there will I give thee my loves. The mandrakes give a smell, and at our gates are all manner of pleasant fruits, new and old, which I have laid up for thee, O my beloved.'

Matthew Henry wrote, 'These are the words of the spouse, the church, the believing soul, in answer to the kind expressions of Christ's love in the preceding verses.'

The church had been without the fellowship of Christ for some time now. He had not neglected her but she had neglected him. His heart had not been cold toward her but her heart had been cold toward him. He had done her no evil but she had done him much evil. He had not forsaken her but she had, for a while, for-saken him. He came to reveal himself, to show his love and grace. He knocked at her door, called to her, and tugged at her heart. But, through her coldness of heart, slothfulness, sin, and desire for ease, she refused him. She withdrew her heart from him, so he withdrew from her the sense of his presence. Though he was always with her, and would never forsake her, she was not aware of his presence.

The sweet manifestation of his love and grace and power were gone (5:2-3).

Even when the Lord hid his face from her and caused her to pass through so much trouble, he acted in love. Her best interest was upon his heart. His purpose was her good. He would prove her love. He was proving her faith. He was making himself more and more precious to her. He was showing her herself, her emptiness, her barrenness, her need of him. Blessed trial!

No sooner had the Lord withdrawn his manifest presence from her, than she realized her shameful neglect and sin. She arose and sought him. Her soul was grieved. Her heart ached with longings for him. She passed through many painful afflictions and trials that were hard to bear. But she continued to love him and to trust him. Her soul was like two armies warring against one another, the one in league with sin, the other in love with Christ. But she continued to seek her Beloved (5:4-8). Is this the condition you are in? How often we bring ourselves into this low condition.

My soul through many changes goes.
His love no variation knows!

At last, the Lord graciously revealed himself to her again. He assured her of his love and grace. He assured her that his heart had not changed. And he promised her that he would come to her again. He said, 'I will go up to the palm tree, I will take hold of the boughs thereof: now also thy breasts shall be as clusters of the vine, and the smell of thy nose like apples' (7:8-9). He said, 'I will come to you again and make myself known unto you. Then, you shall be fruitful. Your soul shall be refreshed.' This promise filled her soul with hope. And this is how she responded to him — 'Come, my beloved.'

Enter our hearts, Redeemer blest,
Enter, thou ever-honoured Guest;
Enter, and make our hearts thine own,
Thy house, thy temple, and thy throne.

And stay, not only for a night,
To bless us with a transient sight;
But with us dwell, through time — and then
In heaven for evermore — Amen.

A blessed assurance of love

Here is a blessed assurance of love. 'I am my beloved's, and his
desire is toward me.' Here we see faith taking Christ at his Word.
He told her of his love for and his interest in her. He told her that
she belonged to him and only to him. And she believed him. Her
heart was made to rejoice in her relation to Christ and her interest
in him. In his name she will boast all the day long (Jer. 9:23-24).

Does your heart enjoy such an assurance of Christ's love? If
you are a sinner trusting Christ alone, you may be sure of this
— You are his, and his desire is toward you! If you love Christ, and
your desire is toward him, you may be sure of this — He loves you,
and his desire is toward you!

'I am my beloved's'

With these words, the believing soul acknowledges that all she is
and all she has belongs to Christ and comes from Christ. And she
here makes a voluntary surrender of all to him again. As she received all from him, she devotes all to him. 'I am my beloved's,'
not my own.

'Ye are not your own, ye are bought with a price'

The Lord Jesus Christ is our Lord. We belong to him. We are his
property. We are his by his own eternal choice (John 15:16). We
are his by legal purchase (Tit. 2:14). We are his by divine gift (John
6:37-39). And we are his by voluntary surrender. Faith in Christ

is nothing less than a voluntary surrender of myself to his dominion (Luke 14:25-33). May the Lord graciously give us continual,
constant devotion to him. We want more than occasional spasms
of devotion. We want continued, unbroken devotion to the Lord
Jesus Christ.

'His desire is toward me.'

As a faithful husband's desire is toward his wife, so that in all things
he seeks her happiness, comfort, and welfare, so Christ's desire is
toward his church. His desire is toward me only. All that the Lord
does, he does for his elect. His desire is toward me from eternity.
His desire is toward me at all times. This is why he came into the
world. 'His desire is toward me.' Before conversion, after conver-
sion, at all times and forever, 'His desire is toward me.' Christ's
desire toward his own elect will never be fully satisfied until he has
them all with him in glory. As a tender husband, the desire of the
Lord's heart is toward his people. He sympathizes with us in all our
distresses. He protects us in all our dangers. And he provides for us
all that we need for time and eternity.

An earnest desire

In verses 11-12, the spouse expresses an earnest desire for her
Beloved. His desire is toward me; and my desire is toward him.
'Come, my beloved, let us go forth into the field; let us lodge in the
villages. Let us get up early to the vineyards.'
       Perhaps, you think, 'The Lord assures us that we are his and
that he will never leave us nor forsake us. That being the case,
such an expression is out of order.' Not so. Is it out of order for a
wife, assured by the experience of her husband's faithful love and
devotion, to constantly yearn for his approving smile? Of course
not. Such yearnings are inspired by the confidence of love rising
from its experience.

Do you long for Christ? Tell him so. 'Come, my beloved.' Let us walk together, that I may receive counsel and instruction from you. Come, comfort my heart, refresh my soul, and revive my spirit. Our Lord walked with the two disciples on the road to Emmaus; and as he talked with them, their hearts burned within them. That experience made them want him all the more. Immediately, they went to the place where they hope to find him, the assembly of his church at Jerusalem (Luke 24:32-36; Matt. 18:20). There they found him.

Having received fresh tokens of his love and fresh assurances of her interest in him, the spouse wanted a better acquaintance with him. She pressed towards 'the excellency of the knowledge of Christ Jesus'. 'Oh, that I may know him', was her cry (Phil. 3:10). We want to know our Saviour doctrinally, experimentally, growingly in the fellowship of his suffering and in the power of his resurrection, being made conformable to him in his death.

She wanted to enjoy personal, private communion with Christ. She wanted to get alone with him. 'Come, my beloved, let us go forth into the field; let us lodge in the villages.' If we would enjoy the fellowship of Christ, we must lay aside the cares and amusements of this world, avoiding everything that would take our hearts away from him (1 Cor. 7:35; Col. 3:1-3). If we would enjoy fellowship with Christ, if we would know him, we must get alone with him. Did our Lord not say, 'When we pray, enter into thy closet, and shut the door'? But, as Matthew Henry put it, 'A believer is never less alone than when he is alone with Christ.'

She was willing to rise early to be with her Lord. She considered it neither trouble nor sacrifice, but a great privilege to do so. She says, 'Let us get up early to the vineyards.' C. H. Spurgeon, commenting on this text, wrote, 'This is put here as the very type and symbol of an earnest and vigorous service for Christ.' It intimates this — If we would enjoy the fellowship and company of Christ, we must be diligent; we must take advantage of our opportunities to hear from, commune with, and worship him. There is nothing particularly excellent, or noble, or spiritual about rising before dawn, but, if we would spend our days with Christ, we must begin our days with Christ. Seek him early; and seek him diligently.

She would be content in any place, under any circumstances, if she could enjoy the presence of Christ with her. What does it take to make us happy and content? Here we see one who was content to take her lodging in the villages, in the huts of the poor, if only Christ would be with her.

> Prisons would palaces prove,
> If Jesus would dwell with me there!

Knowing that earthly comfort and luxury had once nearly stolen her heart, she was willing to make any sacrifice to have her Beloved Saviour's presence. Nothing can satisfy a believing soul but Christ. And nothing can destroy the peace, contentment, and satisfaction of a believer who enjoys the presence and fellowship of Christ.

> All that my soul has tried
> Left but a dismal void;
> Jesus has satisfied,
> Jesus is mine!

When we so desire Christ that we desire nothing but Christ, we shall have Christ (Ps. 73:25).

Examination

In verse 12, the bride, the believing soul, willingly submits to examination by her Beloved. She says, 'Let us see if the vine flourish, whether the tender grape appear, and the pomegranates bud forth.' One reason she desires the presence of Christ is that she may know the state and condition of her own soul (Ps. 139:23-24). Our souls are our vineyards. It is our responsibility to keep our vineyards, not our neighbours' vineyards, but our own, to look after them and examine them. Someone has suggested that the vine is faith, the tender grape hope, and the pomegranates love and joy.

In the examination of our souls, it is always wise to take Christ along. His presence will make the vine to flourish, the tender grape to appear, and the pomegranates to bud forth. As the returning of the sun revives our gardens, the returning of Christ's manifest presence revives our souls. It is to Christ himself that we must appeal for our comfort and assurance, praying like David, 'Say unto my soul, I am thy salvation.'

If he sees the vine of faith flourishing, the tender grape of hope appearing, and the pomegranates of love and joy budding, if we can appeal to him, like Peter, 'Thou knowest all things, thou knowest that I love thee,' if his Spirit bears witness with our spirit that we are the sons of God, that is enough.

Promised love

In verses 12-13, we hear the bride, whose heart has been revived by Christ, making a sincere promise of love to him. 'There', from the depths of my heart and my innermost soul, 'will I give thee my loves. The mandrakes give a smell, and at our gates are all manner of pleasant fruits, new and old, which I have laid up for thee, O my beloved.'

Oh, for grace to give the Lord Jesus Christ all the love of our hearts, so that there is no room left, and nothing left, to give to any rival! This is the sure result of our Lord's reviving presence. When Christ comes and makes himself known to his people, our love and devotion to him is renewed.

Love for Christ must be our motive and our governing principle in all things. 'The love of Christ constraineth us.' He looks beyond our words, and our actions, to the attitude of our hearts. 'All through these verses the spouse acts with reference to her Beloved. It is for him that she goes forth into the field, for the sake of his company, and the quiet enjoyment of his love, she would lodge in the villages; and all manner of pleasant fruits, new and old, which are stored within her gates she declares to be laid up for her Beloved. Love, then, is the fittest and most powerful motive to holy service' (C. H. Spurgeon). This love has about it certain evident peculiarities.

It is a love that realizes the person of the Beloved. The church is strong when the Lord Jesus Christ is real to her. Jesus Christ is not a mere historical person to us, who once lived and died. He is a real person, living today in our midst. He walks among the golden candlesticks, and resides in our souls.

Our love for Christ arises from an assurance of his love for us (1 John 4:19). It is not possible for us to love Christ unless we are made to know that he loves us. When I know that his desire is toward me, then my desire shall be toward him.

Love for Christ leads us to hold all things in joint possession with him. Love is the mother of devotion, sacrifice, and self-denial. Love for Christ causes the believer to give himself and all that he has to Christ. Love does not have divided properties. Such is the love of Christ for us that he gave all that he had for us and gives all that he is and has to us. He could not bear to have anything, not even his throne, that should be altogether for himself. He stripped himself naked to clothe us. Then, he gave us his breath to be our life, and his blood to be our health. Every ransomed soul ought to have such love for Christ that he could sing...

> If I might make some reserve,
> And duty did not call;
> I love my Lord with zeal so great,
> That I would give him all.

Let us more and more have all things in common with our Lord. We are joint-heirs with Christ. All that he has is ours. Let all that we have be his. Our talents, our time, our abilities, our possessions, all are his, rightfully his. Let us constantly live in the awareness that those things we call 'ours' are really his. He has only put them into our hands that we might serve him with them, and serve him with the enjoyment of them.

Love for Christ leads us to go further in serving him. Love for Christ says, 'What more can I do for him?' It is never satisfied with old fruits, it must always bring forth new service for him. Let us bring out everything for him, use it for him, and count it our highest honour that he will accept that which we bring to him.

This love grows and flourishes in the fellowship and communion of Christ. I am afraid that we are far too cold in our love for our altogether lovely Christ, because we live at a distance from him. Oh, may God enable us to live in constant, habitual fellowship and communion with our Saviour. This one thing is needful to promote and sustain revival in our souls. If we have abounding love for Christ, we shall prosper under terrible disadvantages; but if we do not have this love, we have lost the great secret of happiness, peace, and usefulness. Let this be our unceasing prayer and hearts' desire — 'Come, my beloved!'

25.

'I would'

Song of Solomon 8:1-4

'O that thou wert as my brother, that sucked the breasts of my mother! when I should find thee without, I would kiss thee; yea, I should not be despised. I would lead thee, and bring thee into my mother's house, who would instruct me: I would cause thee to drink of spiced wine of the juice of my pomegranate. His left hand should be under my head, and his right hand should embrace me. I charge you, O daughters of Jerusalem, that ye stir not up, nor awake my love, until he please.'

The request of love

This last chapter of this inspired Song of Loves begins with an ardent desire expressed by the church, the Bride of Christ. It is the desire of every believing soul. It is the request of every heart in which the love of Christ is revealed. The request is just this, 'O Lord, give me constant, intimate communion and freedom with you. Let me always know your presence' (Deut. 5:29; Job 23:2; Ps. 14:7). 'O that thou wert as my brother, that sucked the breasts of my mother! when I should find thee without, I would kiss thee; yea, I should not be despised' (v. 1). As Martha sat at the Saviour's feet and heard his word, so the believing heart longs ever to live in communion with him who loved us and gave himself for us, that we may learn of him.

She was already wed to him. He had taken her to be his bride; and she had taken him to be her Lord and husband. Their hearts were already knit together. But the marriage had not yet been publicly solemnized. The marriage feast had not yet been spread. She was obliged, for the sake of decency and respectability, to keep her distance. The bride and her Beloved, when they met in public, could not be so intimate and affectionate as they might desire. Therefore, she wishes that she might be looked upon as his sister, and that she might have the same chaste and innocent familiarity with him that a sister has with her own brother. A brother and a sister who had nursed at the same breasts might be most affectionate, intimate, and free with one another, without any fear of reproach or shame.

This is a prophetic prayer of the Old Testament church for the incarnation of Christ. Our Lord, by means of his incarnation, has really and truly become our Brother. He is not ashamed to call us brethren; and he is made to be the Elder Brother, the Firstborn, of the family of God (Heb. 2:11, 14, 17). We have been adopted as the sons of God (1 John 3:1). His Father is our Father (John 20:17). We, and our Lord are of the same nature and disposition. In the incarnation, he assumed our nature. In regeneration, he gave us his nature.

His love toward us is compared to the love of a brother (Prov. 18:24). Like a brother, he sympathizes with us in all our afflictions. Like a brother, he is touched with the feeling of our infirmities. Like a brother, he helps us in all of our trials. Like a brother, he is tender, compassionate, and caring. The Lord Jesus Christ is a Brother indeed. He is a Brother who is near at hand, ready and willing to help.

This is truly the desire and prayer of every believing heart. Those who know Christ love him. And all who love him desire uninterrupted, intimate communion with him. In essence, this is what she is saying — 'O Lord, when I find you present with me, I will embrace you, kiss you, and show my love to you, as a sister would show her love to her brother. Without shame, I will own you, acknowledge you, and love you, even in the presence of your enemies. I will publicly avow my love to you.'

'I would kiss thee and continue to kiss thee.' Earlier she cried, 'Let him kiss me with the kisses of his mouth: for thy love is better than wine' (1:2; cf. Luke 15:20). Here she longs to kiss him. Those who have been kissed by him in grace wish to kiss him in gratitude. He gave me a kiss of forgiveness; I will give him a kiss of faith. He gave me a kiss of peace; I will give him a kiss of praise. He gave me a kiss of acceptance; I will give him a kiss of adoration. He gave me a kiss of redeeming love; I will give him a kiss of returning love (1 John 4:19).

This text will find its ultimate fulfilment in that day when God's elect shall meet Christ in the clouds. The bride, the Lamb's wife, will not be completely ready until the time of his glorious appearance. But then all his redeemed ones shall be admitted to the nearest possible embraces of Immanuel. With unspeakable pleasure, we will embrace our Redeemer and enjoy him eternally!

'Yea, I should not be despised.' That is to say, 'He will not turn his face away from me, when I reach out to embrace him and kiss him. And those who now despise me will despise me no more. They will envy me.' John Gill pointed out that 'The whole (verse) expresses her boldness in professing Christ, without fear or shame, in the most public manner.'

This is the request of love: 'Let me embrace thee and kiss thee, as a sister would embrace and kiss her beloved brother, without shame or fear.'

The resolve of love

Here is the desire, determination, and resolve of love: 'I would lead thee, and bring thee into my mother's house, who would instruct me: I would cause thee to drink of spiced wine of the juice of my pomegranate' (v. 2). Here, the church, the believing soul, makes

a resolution to improve the opportunity she would have for culti-
vating a more intimate and full knowledge of Christ if she could
always enjoy his communion.

Those who have experienced the goodness, grace, and love of
God in Christ desire others to have the same joyous blessing (Rom.
10:1). 'I would lead thee, and bring thee into my mother's house.'
The believing heart, enjoying personal fellowship and communion
with Christ, says, 'I will bring you into the house of God with me.
My mother, the church of God, and her children need to be acquainted with and enjoy your presence too.' (Compare Galatians
4:26.) As a young woman wants all her family to know and love
her chosen husband, so we want all God's elect to know and enjoy
all the bounty of grace that is ours in Christ. We want the whole
family, our mother and all her children, to enjoy sweet, intimate
communion with Christ, and to experience the blessed influence
of his manifest presence.

All who know Christ should bring him with them into the house
of God, the assembly of his saints (1 Tim. 3:15). When Christ
comes, the dead are made alive, the guilty are forgiven, the fallen
are lifted up, the heavy-hearted are comforted, the troubled are
granted peace, and the fearful are made calm.

Perhaps you think, 'How can I bring the Lord Jesus with me
into the house of God? What can I do to secure the Lord's presence in the midst of his church?' Here the bride speaks of lead-
ing him into her mother's house. Our Saviour must be led, like a
royal king would be led by one of his subjects into his own home.
Would you lead the Lord Jesus Christ into this house? Love him.
Reverence him. Rejoice in him. Call upon him in prayer, asking
him to come with you. You cannot lead him into the assembly of
the saints if you do not come. But do not merely come; come together with God's saints in the house of worship in his name (Matt.
18:20), trusting him, seeking his will and his glory, and the good of
his kingdom. As we thus gather in his name, he promises to meet
with us.

When Christ meets with his people, then the ministry of his
church is profitable and effectual — 'Who would instruct me.' The

allusion here is to a wise mother, who takes her newly wed daughter aside and teaches her how to behave toward her husband, so that she may have his affection and live happily with him. The church, the house of God, is a school of instruction, where souls are taught the ways of Christ, the gospel of Christ, and the will of Christ (Eph. 4:11-16). Believers should always crave such instruction. And that instruction is sure to be profitable and effectual, only when Christ himself is present to teach us by his Spirit (Ps. 45:10-11).

All true, spiritual instruction is instruction from the Word of God, which is able to make us wise unto salvation. It comes through the ministry of God's servants, gospel preachers, pastors according to God's own heart, who feed his people with knowledge and understanding (Jer. 3:15). It is effectually brought to ours hearts by the power of God the Holy Spirit (1 Thess. 1:5).

When the Lord meets with his people, those who know him will offer the sacrifices of their hearts to him (Heb. 13:15). 'I would cause thee to drink of spiced wine of the juice of my pomegranate.' The spiced pomegranate wine was a very rich, flavourful wine, which was delightful to the taste, but less inebriating than other wines. It refers to the graces of the Spirit and the exercise of grace in the believing heart. These are the things that give our Lord pleasure; and are preferred by him to the best of wines (S. of S. 4:10). 'Those that are pleased with Christ', wrote Matthew Henry, 'must study to be pleasing to him; and they will not find him hard to be pleased.' This is the resolve of love. 'I would lead thee and bring thee into my mother's house, both to be instructed by thee and to make my sacrifices of love to thee.'

The rest of love

I hope you can enter into the rest of love described in verse 3. 'His left hand should be under my head, and his right hand should embrace me.' This is one of those texts of Inspiration that is so full of meaning that its depths can hardly be fathomed. Certainly, it speaks of the blessed rest of faith in Christ, who is our Sabbath.

When we come to him and he comes to us, we enter into the blessed rest of love (Heb. 4:9-11). Our Saviour's embrace implies his love of us. Our willingness to be and desire to be embraced by him speaks of our love for him. 'We love him because he first loved us.' Being embraced in his omnipotent arms, we are assured of his unfailing support. 'Underneath are the everlasting arms.' In those arms of almighty goodness, grace, and love we are safe and secure. No evil shall befall us in his arms. This is our place of confident rest, and it is glorious (Isa. 11:10). When our Lord reveals himself and makes his presence known, our hearts are at peace. We rest in him!

The responsibility of love

All privileges bring responsibility. Our Lord has come to us. He has granted to us his presence in this place. 'His left hand is under my head; and his right hand doth embrace me.' It is our great joy and privilege in this place to rest in his love. Now, 'I charge you, O daughters of Jerusalem, that you stir not up, nor awake my love till he please.' So long as our Lord is pleased to dwell in our midst, let us be careful not to disturb him, grieve him, and drive him away (Eph. 4:30). Remember what it is like to be without him (S. of S. 5:6). Remember the evil that grieved him before (5:1-6). Remember always to remember him, honour him, and embrace him in the arms of faith, gratitude, and love, and kiss him with the lips of prayer.

26.

Leaning on Christ

Song of Solomon 8:5-7

'Who is this that cometh up from the wilderness, leaning upon her beloved? I raised thee up under the apple tree: there thy mother brought thee forth: there she brought thee forth that bare thee. Set me as a seal upon thine heart, as a seal upon thine arm: for love is strong as death; jealousy is cruel as the grave: the coals thereof are coals of fire, which hath a most vehement flame. Many waters cannot quench love, neither can the floods drown it: if a man would give all the substance of his house for love, it would utterly be contemned.'

Faith in Christ is described by many symbolic actions. Faith toward Christ has nothing whatsoever to do with physical acts, physical posture, or physical movement. But, in the Word of God, faith is described symbolically by many actions of the body.

Faith is looking to Christ and seeing him. He says, 'Behold me, behold me...Look unto me and be ye saved all the ends of the earth, for I am God and there is none else' (Isa. 45:1, 22). Our Lord says, 'This is the will of him that sent me, that everyone which seeth the Son, and believeth on him may have everlasting life' (John 6:40). Saving faith is looking to Christ, like the perishing Israelites looked to the brazen serpent and were healed.

Faith is coming to Christ. 'He that cometh to me shall never hunger; and he that believeth on me shall never thirst' (John 6:35). 'Come unto me, all ye that labour and are heavy-laden, and I will give you rest' (Matt. 11:28). 'All that the Father giveth me shall come to me; and him that cometh unto me, I will in no wise cast out' (John 6:37). Saving faith is coming to Christ, acknowledging him as Lord and trusting him as Saviour. We come to you, our Saviour, for pardon, for redemption, for righteousness, for life. We have come to him. We are coming to him. And we shall yet come to him.

Faith is fleeing to Christ. We have 'fled for refuge to lay hold on the hope set before us' (Heb. 6:18). Christ, 'the Lord is a strong tower; the righteous runneth into it, and is safe' (Prov. 18:10). Realizing that were are under the wrath of God, and knowing that the Lord Jesus Christ is God's only appointed place of refuge for guilty sinners, we flee to him. We venture our souls on him, on the merits of his blood and righteousness. We cast ourselves into his arms of power and grace, trusting him alone to save us. Saving faith is fleeing to Christ in hope of mercy.

Faith is laying hold of Christ. Like a drowning man lays hold of the line thrown to him, we lay hold of Christ and cling to him.

Faith is receiving Christ. 'As many as received him, to them gave he power to become the sons of God, even to them that believe on his name' (John 1:12). It is not receiving Christ into the head that brings salvation, but receiving him into the heart. It is not receiving the doctrine of Christ that saves us, but receiving Christ himself. A person may acknowledge all the truth revealed about Christ and yet not trust him. Judas did not reject Christ's doctrine. Yet, he despised him. True faith receives the whole Christ as he is revealed in Holy Scripture. We receive him in all his offices, for the whole of our acceptance before God, in all his teaching (doctrine), and in preference to all others.

But in this passage we see faith described in richer, fuller, more intimate connection. 'Who is this that cometh up out of the wilderness, leaning upon her beloved?' Here is faith, but it is something more than 'looking for life', or 'coming in hope', or 'fleeing for mercy', or 'laying hold of help', or even 'receiving a Saviour'. This is intimate, confident, loving, admiring, adoring faith leaning on Christ. Here is a description of the church of God and of every true believer. The people of God are as a bride coming up out of a dark, dangerous, and desolate wilderness, leaning upon her Beloved, the Lord Jesus Christ.

Leaning

First, we see faith leaning. 'Who is this that cometh up out of the wilderness, leaning upon her beloved?' There is no better description of true faith than the picture of a sinner leaning on Christ. Like a cripple man leans on his crutches, the children of God lean on Christ. Like a timid, frightened women, passing through some strange and dangerous forest at night, might lean upon the strong arm of her husband, we lean upon our Beloved. We lean upon him, because he has proven his love for us and his faithfulness to us. We lean upon him, because he is mighty and able to protect us. There is a clear connection between the sweet fellowship with Christ described in verses 1-4 and faith in Christ. The more we trust him, the more heavily we lean upon him, the more constant and real our fellowship will be.

Some suggest that this question was raised by Christ. But it seems most likely to me that it is a question raised by the daughters of Jerusalem, when the Shulamite had solemnly charged them not to disturb her Beloved.

The people of God in this world are passing through a wilderness. To the heavenly pilgrim, this world is a barren and desolate wilderness. Sometimes our pathway leads us through rivers of woe, deep waters of affliction, and seas of temptation. There are many dangers to be overcome, many snares to avoid, and many enemies to face. The world, the flesh, and the devil oppose us. The lust of the eye, the lust of the flesh, and the pride of life make our journey a troublesome one. But onward we must go.

Don't ever forget, child of God, we are only pilgrims here. Be sure that your heart is fixed upon Immanuel's land, and not upon the things of this world (Heb. 11:8-10, 14-16; 1 John 2:15-17; Col. 3:1-3). But our pilgrimage is not a lonely one. The Bride is not alone. Her Beloved is with her. Every soul that journeys toward heaven has Christ for its companion. Our Lord allows no pilgrim to the New Jerusalem to travel alone. Christ is with us in tender, deeply felt sympathy. Whatever our temptations may be, he has been tempted in every point, just as we are. Whatever our afflictions may be, he has been so afflicted. He is touched with the feeling of our infirmities. Our Saviour is also with us in reality (Isa. 43:2-5; 41:10). He is always at hand (Phil. 4:4). This is not a dream, or a piece of fiction. It is fact, a blessed, glorious fact. 'The Lord is at hand!' And though our pilgrimage sometimes seems long, we are passing through this bleak land. 'Who is this that cometh up from the wilderness?' We shall not be in this wilderness forever.

> Through many dangers, toils, and snares
> I have already come:
> 'Tis grace that brought me safe thus far,
> And grace will lead me home.

Throughout our pilgrimage here, it is our privilege and joy to be leaning on Christ, 'Leaning on her Beloved.'

> Learning to lean, learning to lean
> I'm learning to lean on Jesus;
> Finding more power than I'd ever dreamed,
> I'm learning to lean on Jesus.

Do you know anything about this posture of faith? Do you know anything about leaning on Christ? That is what faith is, it is leaning on Christ. Faith leans on Christ for all things and at all times. 'Trust in the LORD with all thine heart; and lean not unto thine own understanding. In all thy ways acknowledge him, and he shall direct thy paths' (Prov. 3:5-6). Trust Christ, lean on him for all

your salvation, for all things relating to daily providence, and for all
things regarding the future.

> Every hour of everyday,
> Every moment, and in every way,
> I'm leaning on Jesus, he's the Rock of my soul,
> I'm singing his praises wherever I go!

The bride leans upon her Beloved. Christ is the Beloved. He
is Beloved of the Father. He is Beloved of the angels. He is Beloved of the saints in heaven. He is the Beloved of every saved,
believing soul. Is the Lord Jesus Christ your Beloved? (1 Pet. 2:7; 1
Cor. 16:22). There is no better description of faith than leaning on
Christ. We lean on the person of Christ for acceptance with God.
We lean on the righteousness of Christ for justification. We lean on
the blood of Christ for pardon and cleansing. We lean on the fulness of Christ to supply all our needs, both physical and spiritual,
temporal and eternal (Lam. 3:23-26).

In prayer, we lean on Christ. In worship, we lean on Christ. In
giving, we lean on Christ. In praise, we lean on Christ. All our hope
of acceptance with God is Christ, so we lean on him. Oh, may we
evermore learn to lean heavily upon the Son of God. Go ahead
and lean on him! He can bear all the weight of your soul.

This word 'leaning' has many shades of meaning. It suggests
a picture of the bride casting herself upon her Beloved, joining
herself to her Beloved, associating with her Beloved, cleaving to
her Beloved, rejoicing in her Beloved, strengthening herself in her
Beloved, and clinging to, or hanging onto her Beloved. This is the
posture of faith. 'Leaning upon her Beloved.'

Remembering

Second, we see faith remembering. 'I raised thee up under the
apple tree: there thy mother brought thee forth: there she brought
the forth that bare thee' (v. 5). Reading only the English translation,

we would assume that these words were spoken by Christ to the church. But in the Hebrew, the pronoun 'thee' is masculine. So again, the bride is speaking to her Beloved.

She remembers the past. 'I raised thee up.' That is to say, I have sought thee in prayer and prevailed upon thee to help me and to comfort me (Ps. 44:23; 34:1-6). Like the disciples raised Christ up to help them in the storm, crying, 'Master, carest thou not that we perish?' the children of God raise him up in prayer.

He is ready and willing to yield to our importunate cries of faith. Out of the bitter pains of conviction and repentance, Christ is found in the soul and brought forth in travail, like a son born of his mother's travail into the world. Out of the depths of desperate need, agony of soul and heaviness of heart, believing sinners cry out to Christ in times of trouble and raise him up to help.

The bride here looks to the future. Christ came in the first advent, in his incarnation, being conceived in and born into this world out of the womb of the Old Testament church (Rev. 12:1-17). Our Lord himself uses this metaphor to describe the joy his people will have at his second advent (John 16:21-22).

Praying

Third, we see faith praying (v. 6). 'Set me as a seal upon thine heart, as a seal upon thine arm.' As she makes her pilgrimage through this world, she prays that her union with him might be confirmed, that her communion with him might be constant, and that her fellowship with him might be intimate.

Each of us, as believers, might very well take these same words to express the prayer and desire of our hearts. 'Set me as a seal upon thine heart, as a seal upon thine arm.'

Let me have a place in your heart and an interest in your love. The allusion is to the High Priest (Exod. 28:11, 12, 21, 29, 30). It is enough for me, and all I desire, that Christ be my sin-atoning High Priest, that he carry me upon his heart when he stands before God. Let me never lose the place that I have in your heart. Let your love be secured to me, as a deed that is sealed cannot be broken (Eph. 1:14; 4:30). Let me always be near and dear to you. 'Set me as a seal upon thine arm.' The allusion here is to those bracelets that young lovers wear with the name of their sweethearts engraved upon them (Isa. 49:13-16). Let your power be engaged for me as token of your love for me. Oh my Beloved, defend me and protect me with the right arm of your power!

Persevering

Fourth, we see faith persevering (vv. 6-7). 'Set me as a seal upon thine heart, as a seal upon thine arm: for love is strong as death; jealousy is cruel as the grave: the coals thereof are coals of fire, which hath a most vehement flame. Many waters cannot quench love, neither can the floods drown it: if a man would give all the substance of his house for love, it would utterly be contemned.'

All true faith is persevering faith. It perseveres in love for Christ. If ever a man comes to know and love the Lord Jesus Christ, he will continue in both faith and love toward him. Love for Christ is the vigorous passion of the believing heart. It is strong as death. His love for us was stronger than death. And the love of true believer for Christ is as strong as death. Love for Christ makes the believer dead to everything else.

Jealousy is cruel as the grave. We are jealous of anything that might draw us away from him, because we love him. We are jealous of ourselves, lest we should do anything to provoke him to leave us. Love for Christ is an all-consuming fire in the hearts of his children.

Love for Christ is the victorious passion of the believing heart (v. 7). 'Many waters cannot quench love, neither can the floods drown it: if a man would give all the substance of his house for love, it would utterly be contemned.' Neither the substance of this world nor the swelling floods of death could quench our Saviour's love for us (Rom. 8:38-39). And where there is true love for Christ, it cannot be destroyed. Waters of affliction cannot quench love. It only grows stronger. Floods of trouble cannot destroy love. It only clings more firmly to its object. All the riches of the world cannot buy love. Even life itself would be despised, before love could be sacrificed.

May the Lord graciously grant us this holy faith and this love for Christ that rises from it! May his love constantly be shed abroad in our hearts by the Holy Spirit and constantly inspire and constrain us to lean upon him as the solitary Object of our souls' faith and love.

27.

A choice prayer for saints and sinners

Song of Solomon 8:6-7

'Set me as a seal upon thine heart, a seal upon thine arm: for love is strong as death; jealousy is cruel as the grave: the coals thereof are coals of fire, which hath a most vehement flame. Many waters cannot quench love, neither can the floods drown it.'

What a description this is of the love of Christ, the 'love that passeth knowledge'. It is Christ who says, 'I have loved thee with an everlasting love, and with loving-kindness have I drawn thee.' It is God our Saviour who declares, 'I drew them with cords of love, and with the bands of a man.' He found us in a desert land, and in a waste howling wilderness. 'Christ loved the church, and gave himself for it.'

The Lord Jesus here declares his love to his church, and she replies, 'set me as a seal', not only on thy heart, but also on your arm — the place of your love and the place of your strength — the place of the most tender emotion and deepest passion, and the place of power, safety, and work.

Who shall separate us from the love of Christ? His love is invincible and irresistible as death. It is a jealous love, as unyielding and unalterable as the grave. Its comparable to fire, coals of fire, the very flame of Jehovah. Here, then, is the love of Christ! Its breadth, length, height, and depth, are absolutely immeasurable.

Our fear

This is not the prayer of a soul that is longing for fellowship. That prayer is, 'Tell me, O thou whom my soul loveth, where thou feedest.' This is not even the prayer of the soul that has some fellowship, but longs for more. Then the prayer would be, 'O that thou wert as my brother!' And this is not the prayer of one that once enjoyed the fellowship of Christ, but has now lost it. That cry would be, 'Saw ye him whom my soul loveth?' Then the sorrowful soul goes about the streets of the city, saying, 'I will seek him, for I am sick of love.'

This is the prayer of the believing soul who has the present enjoyment of Christ's fellowship, but is fearful that the sweet communion might be interrupted. Therefore, the spouse here pleads for something that would be to her a token of the covenant between her and her Beloved when his manifest presence might be withdrawn. This is the prayer of the spouse when she has been coming up out of the wilderness, leaning upon her Beloved. The thought seems to strike her that he who has sustained her is about to be taken from her for a season because it is expedient and more useful for her. Therefore, she prays that, before he leaves the earth and enters again into his heavenly kingdom, he might be pleased to enter into a covenant with her, never to forget her, and that he might give her some sign and pledge of his love to her. She wanted to know that she would always be near to his heart while she waited for his return.

I take this to be the prayer of the church in this present gospel age. Today Christ is before his Father's throne. The Bridegroom is no longer with us physically. His bodily presence has been taken from us. He has, in that sense, left us. He has gone to heaven to prepare a place for us. He told us that he must go away, and that his going away was expedient for us (John 16:7). But he promised that he would come again, and that when he returns we will be together with him forever (John 14:1-3). Today we long for his coming.

In the language of the last verse of this Holy Song of Love, we say, 'Make haste, my beloved, and be thou like to a roe or to a young hart upon the mountains of spices.' Or, in the language of the Revelation, we hear him say, 'Surely I come quickly.' And our hearts respond, 'Amen. Even so, come, Lord Jesus!' Yet, before he went away, as we read the gospel narratives, it seems as though his church was saying, 'Set me as a seal upon thine heart, as a seal upon thine arm.' This is the prayer of God's church today. Though our Lord's bodily presence is absent from us, we want to be near him, near his heart, and we want to have the blessed conscious-ness of the fact that we are upon his heart.

I ask my dying Saviour dear
To set me on his heart;
And if my Jesus fix me there,
Nor life, nor death shall part.

As Aaron bore upon his breast
The names of Jacob's sons,
So bear my name among the rest
Of thy dear chosen ones.

But seal me also with thine arm,
Or yet I am not right.
I need thy love to ward off harm,
And need thy shoulder's might.

This double seal makes all things sure,
And keeps me safe and well;
Thy heart and shoulder will secure
From all the host of hell.

Our prayer

This is a prayer that arises from the earnest hearts of God's believing children. Yet, it is a prayer any sinner desiring mercy, grace, and salvation might make at the throne of grace. 'Set me as a seal upon thine heart, as a seal upon thine arm.' The allusion here is, as I have shown you, to the high priest in Israel. The prayer is really twofold. She longs to know that she has an interest in the love of Christ's heart, and she longs to experience the power of his arm (Exod. 28:12, 29-30, 36-38).

Believers know the meaning of this prayer by personal experience. It is the longing, the desire of a sinner seeking grace to know that his name is engraved upon the Saviour's heart. In the language of the psalmist, we say to the Lord Jesus, 'Say unto my soul, I am thy salvation.' I desire an interest in your love; but I want more. I want to know that I have an interest in your love. Write my name in your heart, and engrave it as a signet upon your heart, so that I may see it and know it.

Without question, there are many whose names are written on our Lord's heart who do not yet know it. Christ has loved them from all eternity. His heart has been set upon them from everlasting. But they have not yet seen the signet with their names written upon it.

In all of his work our great High Priest bears the names that are upon his heart. For them he makes intercession (John 17:9, 20; 1 John 2:1-2). He bore their sins in his body upon the cursed tree (1 Pet. 2:24; 3:18), and endured all the wrath of divine judgement to the full satisfaction of justice for them (Isa. 53:9-11). He made atonement for them, putting away their sins by the sacrifice of himself (Heb. 9:26). He obtained eternal redemption for them by the merit of his blood (Heb. 9:12). Upon them he pronounces the blessing of God (Num. 6:24-27; Eph. 1:3-6).

We want to know, to experience the power of our Saviour's arm. We want always to see and know that our Redeemer's heart and hand are eternally engaged for us, engaged to accomplish our everlasting salvation. This is our souls desire. We want to know and be assured that the Lord Jesus Christ is our High Priest, our Advocate, our sin-atoning Mediator before God. If we can know that we have a place in his heart of love and that his arm is set to do us good, we want no more. All is well with our souls. His arm preserves us, protects us, and provides for us. This is the prayer we make. What more could we desire than this? 'Set me as a seal upon thine heart, as a seal upon thine arm.'

Our plea

Anytime we go to God in prayer, it is wise to not only make our request known to him, but also to offer a plea, an argument, a reason why he should grant the thing we ask. Be sure that you understand this: The only grounds upon which we can appeal to God for mercy are to be found in God himself (See Ps. 51:1-5). Our hope, our basis of appeal with God must be found in him.

See how the spouse here urges her request. She says, 'Make me to know your love for me, because I know this concerning your love: It is as strong as death — It is as firm as the grave — It is as intense as fire — It is as unquenchable as eternity.' With these four pleas she backs up and presses her suit for mercy.

Show me your love, for your love is strong as death. 'Love is strong as death.' The love of Christ is as irresistible as death. The love of Christ triumphed over death for us. As death refuses to give up its victims, so the love of Christ refuses to give up its captives. Nothing shall ever cause the Son of God to cease loving his people and let them go.

Show me your love, for your love is as firm as the grave.' Jealousy is cruel as the grave.' These words would be more accurately translated, 'Jealousy is as hard as hell.' Our Lord is jealous over his people. He will not allow those whom he loves to be taken from him. You will more likely see the gates of hell opened, the fires of hell quenched, and the spirits of the damned set free, than see the Son of God lose one of those who are engraved upon his heart (Rom. 8:28-39). Those whom God has chosen, he will never refuse. Those Christ has redeemed, he will never sell. Those he has justified, he will never condemn. Those he has found, he will never lose. Those he has loved, he will never hate.

Show me your love, for your love is as intense as fire. 'The coals thereof are coals of fire, which hath a most vehement flame.' These words seem to allude to that fire which always burned at the altar and never went out. Those coals of fire were always kept burning in the typical Levitical dispensation. The flame was originally kindled by God. It was the work of the priests to perpetually feed it with the sacred fuel. The love of Christ is like the coals of that altar which never went out, and more. The love of Christ for his own elect is vehement, blazing, intense love that never diminishes. The only cause of his love for us is in himself. There is nothing, no form of love to compare with his love. The love of Christ for his elect is free, sovereign, eternal, saving, immutable love.

Show me your love, for your love is as unquenchable as eternity. 'Many waters cannot quench love, neither can the floods drown it' (Rom. 8:37-39). No other love is really unquenchable, but our Saviour's love is. His love is eternal and everlasting, immutable and unalterable. The love of Christ is infinitely beyond that of a father or a mother, or a brother or a sister, or a husband or a wife. The love of Christ is the one and only love that passes knowledge, the one love that nothing in heaven, or earth, or hell is able to extinguish or cool, the one love whose dimensions are beyond all measure (Eph. 3:14-19).

Our Redeemer's love is here compared to fire that cannot be quenched. As such it is affirmed that 'waters', 'many waters' cannot quench it. Christ's love for us is something the floods cannot drown (Ps. 69:15; 93:3). The waters of God's wrath could not quench the love of Christ for his people. 'Having loved his own which were in the world, he loved them to the end.' It was our Saviour's matchless love for us that made him willing to endure all the horror of God's wrath in our stead.

The waters of shame and suffering sought to quench and drown it. They would have hindered its outflowing, and come (like Peter) between the Saviour and the cross, but his love refused to be quenched on its way to Calvary. Herein was love! It leaped over all the barriers in its way. It refused to be extinguished or drowned. Its fire would not be quenched. Its life could not be drowned (Ps. 69:1-7).

The waters of death sought to quench it. The waves and billows of death went over the great Lover of our souls. The grave sought to cool or quench his love; but it proved itself stronger than death. Neither death nor the grave could alter or weaken his love for us. It came out of both death and the grave as strong as before. Love defied death, and overcame it.

Even the floods of our sins could not quench the love of Christ for us. The waters of our unworthiness could not quench nor drown the love of Christ for our souls. Love is usually attracted to that which is loveable. When something ugly, unlovely, unattractive comes love (as it is called) withdraws from its object. Not so here. All our unfitness and unloveableness could not quench nor drown the love of Christ. It clings to the unlovely, and refuses to be torn away.

The waters of our long rejection sought to quench it. Though the gospel showed us that personal unworthiness could not arrest the love of Christ, we continued to reject him and his love. We continued to hate him and despise his love. Yet, his love for us rose above our enmity to him, rose above our unbelief, and survived our hardness. In spite of everything we are and have done, his love was unquenched.

Though he has saved us by his matchless grace, the waters of our daily inconsistency seek to quench his love, but blessed be his name, without success! Even after experiencing his adorable grace, we are constantly spurning his unspurnable love! What inconsistencies, coldness, lukewarmness, unbelief, worldliness, hardness, and utter ungodliness daily flows from us against the Saviour's love like a mighty flood to quench its fire and drown its life! Yet it survives all; it remains unquenched, unquenchable and unchanged!

All these infinite evils in us are like 'waters', 'many waters', like 'floods', torrents of sin, waves and billows of evil, all constantly labouring to quench and drown the love of Christ! They would annihilate any other love, any love less than his. But our Saviour's love is unchangeable and everlasting.

28.

Unpurchasable love

Song of Solomon 8:7

'If a man would give all the substance of his house for love, it would be utterly contemned.'

Love is unpurchasable. That is a general truth, which may be applied to every form of true love. You cannot purchase love. True love cannot be bought nor sold. It is free, spontaneous, and faithful. I am not talking about the silly, sentimental passions and emotions that people call love. That is bought and sold at a very cheap price. It is as fickle as water. But true love, that love that is self-denying, self-sacrificing, and devoted, that love which is more interested in its object than it is in self, true love cannot be purchased; and it cannot be sold. 'Love is strong as death…Many waters cannot quench love, neither can the floods drown it.' Love is both free and faithful. It cannot be bought; and it cannot be destroyed.

The love of a husband or wife cannot be purchased. Every young man and young lady, who is wise, will lay this fact to heart. You cannot buy the love of a husband. You cannot buy the love of a wife. Many homes would be much happier if there were a tithe as much love as there is wealth. It takes more than money, reputation, social standing, and luxury to build a home. A home is a place where love dwells. A home is a place where love is felt, expressed, and active. Many times, love will come in the poor man's door, making his home a bright and happy place, when it cannot enter the luxury of the rich.

Who could purchase a mother's love? She loves her own child especially, because it is her own child. She watches over her baby with care. She denies herself necessary sleep at night if her baby is sick. She would be ready to part with her life at a moment's notice to spare the fruit of her womb. Bring another woman's child, and endow her with great wealth to induce her to love it; and you will find that it is not in her power to transfer her love from her own child to the son or daughter of another. Her own child is exceedingly precious to her. Another infant, that to an eye unprejudiced by love might be far more beautiful, can never receive the love that belongs to her own. Offer her any price; it would be utterly despised. Love cannot be purchased.

Even the love of friends is without price. I am showing you that the language of this text applies to every form of true love. The love of Jonathan and David for one another was so great that they entered into a covenant with one another. David did not buy Jonathan's love, or Jonathan David's. And no price could purchase their hearts from one another. It may or may not be true that 'every man has his price;' but love has no price. No, if a man should give all the substance of his house even for human love, for the common love that exists between man and man, it would be utterly despised.

But here the Holy Spirit speaks of a much higher love. All that I have said about love is pre-eminently true when we come to think of the love of Christ for us, and when we think of that love which springs up in the human heart for the Lord Jesus Christ when the Spirit of God has renewed our hearts and shed abroad the love of God in our souls. Neither the love of Christ for us, nor the love of our hearts for him can be purchased. If a man should offer to give all the substance of his house for either of these forms of love, it would be utterly despised.

Christ's love for us — unpurchasable

We will begin at the highest point and the original source of all true love. The love of the Lord Jesus Christ for his people cannot be purchased. Our Saviour is no mercenary. He does not auction his love and grace to the highest bidder. It would be a profane and monstrous blasphemy to suppose that the love of his heart could be bought with silver, gold, and earthly stores.

If anything could enrage the heart of the eternal God, I am sure it would be the attempts of men to purchase his love and the favours of his love by what they suppose they do for him or give to him. The pride and stupidity of man is so great that he dares to suppose that the love of God is for sale, like the love of a common prostitute. Paul very plainly tells us that those preachers who are peddlers of self-righteousness who preach up law and works, as a basis of salvation, are nothing more than prostitutes. They have prostituted the gospel of Christ (Compare Phil. 3:2 and Deut. 23:18). The love of Christ is not for sale!

If it were, what do you suppose you might give him to buy his love? He has need of nothing. Everything in the vast universe belongs to him (Ps. 50:7-12). There is nothing, which he conceives in his infinite mind, that he could not fashion at once by his mighty power. There is nothing his heart could desire that he cannot command to appear before him.

What do you suppose you might do for Christ to win his love? What proud worms we are to think that by giving or doing anything, we can win the love and favour of the infinite God. He is not like us. His love is not for sale. His favours cannot be purchased. The Almighty cannot be bribed.

If the love of Christ could be won by us by something we might give or do for him, then it must be concluded that our works and our gifts are of equal merit and of equal value with his love. That cannot be. The silver and gold, which we so highly treasure, is nothing more to the Son of God than the gravel in your driveway. As Augustus Toplady wrote, 'Christ loved money so little, that he had but one thief, and he made him his purse-bearer.'

In time of pain and trouble, in heaviness and sorrow, in sickness, bereavement, and death, try to find comfort for your soul in your works or in your gifts if you dare. You will find them to be a source of torment for your conscience, but never will they bring comfort to your soul. Nothing can give our souls peace and comfort, except a saving knowledge of the love of God in Christ. If these things will not satisfy you, they certainly will not satisfy God!

There is no emotion we have ever felt in our most sanctified moments, there is no holy desire that has ever passed through our hearts in our most hallowed times, there is no heavenly longing that has been begotten in our souls by the Spirit of God, that we should dare to put side by side with the love of Christ, and say, 'This is worthy of my Saviour's love.'

Everything we have belongs to Christ already. Everything we could possibly do for Christ, we are already lawfully obliged to do for him.

Yet, though we could never purchase the love of Christ by any price, every believing sinner, saved by God's free grace has his love in all its infinite fulness. Child of God, rejoice! The Son of God loves us. He has freely bestowed upon us what he never would have sold us, what we never could have purchased from him. He said, 'I will love them freely' (Hosea 14:4), and he does. He has bestowed his love upon us freely, 'Without money and without price.'

His love for us is an eternal and everlasting love (Jer. 31:3). His love for us is a sovereign and free love (Rom. 9:13). His love for us is a self-sacrificing, redeeming, saving love (1 John 4:9-10). His love for us is an immutable and indestructible love (Mal. 3:6). His love for us arises entirely from within himself. The source, the spring, the cause of our Saviour's love for us is in his own holy Being.

Here is the greatest marvel in all the world to me —This unpurchasable love, this eternal, unending love is mine. 'He loved me and gave himself for me!' You, my brother, my sister, if you have been saved by his grace, can always say, 'This love is mine.

The Lord Jesus Christ loves me with a love that I never could have purchased.'

Truly, the love of Christ passeth knowledge. It is, like himself, infinite. It emerges out of every storm or flood. It survives all unworthiness, and unbelief, and rejection. It is this that fills the soul, that liberates us from bondage that gladdens our hearts in the most sorrowful hour. Love is the true sunshine of life; and with this love Christ is to fill, not heaven only, but also earth when he comes again in his glory.

Perhaps the one who reads these lines might think, 'O how I wish I could have the love of Christ in my heart.' If you really do want the love of Christ, let this word from God guide you into the way by which you may know the love of Christ. Do not try to purchase the love of Christ; abandon that foolish notion at once. Receive the love of Christ as a free-gift, for which you are utterly unworthy, by simply trusting him.

Our love for Christ — unpurchasable

As Christ's love for us could never be purchased, the believer's love for Christ is not purchased, not even by all the Lord's many gifts to us. It is true, 'We love him, because he first loved us.' The Lord's love for us caused our love for him. And we are and should be grateful for the many gifts of love he has so freely and bounteously bestowed upon us. But the true believer does not love Christ because of all the gifts his love has given us.

Satan's accusation against Job was false (Job 1:8-12, 20-21; 2:3-10). The believer's love for Christ does not vary and alter according to our temporal circumstances. Our love for Christ does not vary with our spiritual experiences (S. of S. 5:8, 10-16). Even the many blessings of grace, which Christ has given us, are not the cause of our love to him.

It is the Lord Jesus Christ himself that we love, not the things he gives us. There are several small items I possess that are precious to me. They would not be, except for one thing; they were given to me by people who love me and by people I love. In much the same way, we cherish our Saviour's gifts to us because they are his gifts; but the Object of our love is Christ himself.

Christ himself has won our hearts. I believe all the doctrines of the grace of God: election, redemption, justification, and re-generation. I rejoice in all the blessings of grace: forgiveness, righ-teousness, adoption, salvation, and eternal life. I rest in the blessed promises of grace: resurrection, glorification, heaven, and eternal glory. But the love of my heart is reserved for Christ alone. I love him. All these other things are the substance of his house. They could never have won my heart until Christ himself was revealed in my heart by the Holy Spirit.

'My beloved is mine, and I am his.' I am truly thankful to know that his crown is mine, his throne is mine, his home is mine, his grace is mine, and his name is mine. But it is Christ himself who charms and wins my heart. Christ himself is mine. And I am his.

No substitute for love

Our Lord Jesus Christ will accept no substitute for love. The Lord God says to each of his children, 'My son, give me thine heart' (Prov. 23:26). There are many who wish to think they are God's children who will give him anything, but love. Man will offer God anything, except that which has to do with the heart. A man will say, or do, or give most anything except bow his heart to God.

Until you give Christ the love of your heart, you will never be accepted by him (Luke 14:25-27, 33). We receive the Saviour by faith in him, not by love for him. But faith in him causes love for him. Any faith that does not bring with it true love for the Son of God is false faith.

The believing heart is motivated by love for Christ. Unless love for Christ is the motive and principle of our worship, our service, and our gifts to him, he will never accept them or us (2 Cor. 9:7).

Love is a better motive than law. It does more. It gives more. It produces more. Love is devotion. Love withholds nothing. Love gives all.

Here is a point of examination. I have challenged, searched, and tried my own heart by these questions. I call upon you to do the same. Would I do more for Christ than I am now doing for him if I thought it would have any bearing on my eternal salvation? Would my worship, devotion and faithfulness to Christ be any more sincere if I felt that my eternal salvation depended upon it? Would I give more to Christ of my time, my talents, or my money if I thought that by doing so I would gain greater riches in this world, or greater reward in heaven, or if I feared that God might punish me for giving so little as I do?

In other words, would I be more faithful to Christ than I now am if I truly felt in my heart that my salvation and my eternal relationship with God depended upon the works of the law, rather than upon his free grace? Of this I am sure — If the threat of punishment or the promise of reward could persuade a person to do more, give more, or behave better than the constraint of love, that person is utterly void of the grace of God (1 Cor. 16:22). I repeat, it is not love for Christ that brings salvation. Faith brings us into a saving union with Christ. But where there is a heart faith in Christ, there is a heart love for Christ.

But those who truly love Christ will not sell their love for him at any price. Offer them what you will. Bribe them with money. Bribe them with imprisonment. Bribe them with their lives. The price that you offer would be utterly despised. True love is not for sale. 'If a man would give all the substance of his house for love, it would utterly be contemned.' By this test we will prove what we are. True love cannot be purchased.

Our Saviour would never give us anything as a substitute for love. Let us never attempt to give our Saviour anything as a substitute for love. Though we give our body to be burned, what would that be without love? If we bring him gifts, offerings, prayers, tears, money, everything but love, we bring him nothing. Without love, what are the riches of the universe? It is love that our Saviour gives. It is love he wants from us. What shall be given in exchange for love?

Not for sale

'If a man would give all the substance of his house for love, it would be utterly contemned.' Look at this from another angle. The believer's love for Christ can never be purchased at any price. It is not for sale. As his love for us is not for sale, so the love of our hearts for the Lord Jesus Christ is not for sale.

I have seen many sell their professed love for Christ at a very cheap price. There are many Esaus among God's professed people who are ready and willing to make a deal with Satan to sell their birthright for a bowl of soup. There are many Judases among the saints who are quite willing to sell their Master for thirty pieces of silver.

> I love the LORD, because he hath heard my voice and my supplications. Because he hath inclined his ear unto me, therefore will I call upon him as long as I live. The sorrows of death compassed me, and the pains of hell gat hold upon me: I found trouble and sorrow. Then called I upon the name of the LORD; O LORD, I beseech thee, deliver my soul. Gracious is the LORD, and righteous; yea, our God is merciful. The LORD preserveth the simple: I was brought low, and he helped me. Return unto thy rest, O my soul; for the LORD hath dealt bountifully with thee...O LORD, truly I am thy servant; I am thy servant, and the son of thine handmaid: thou hast loosed my bonds. I will offer to thee the sacrifice of thanksgiving, and will call upon the name of the LORD (Ps. 116:1-7, 16-17).

'We love him, because he first loved us' (1 John 4:19).

'Keep yourselves in the love of God, looking for the mercy of our Lord Jesus Christ unto eternal life' (Jude 1:21).

29.

Our sister, our service, our Savior

Song of Solomon 8:8-14

'We have a little sister, and she hath no breasts: what shall we do for our sister in the day when she shall be spoken for? If she be a wall, we will build upon her a palace of silver: and if she be a door, we will enclose her with boards of cedar. I am a wall, and my breasts like towers: then was I in his eyes as one that found favour. Solomon had a vineyard at Baalhamon; he let out the vineyard unto keepers; every one for the fruit thereof was to bring a thousand pieces of silver. My vineyard, which is mine, is before me: thou, O Solomon, must have a thousand, and those that keep the fruit thereof two hundred. Thou that dwellest in the gardens, the companions hearken to thy voice: cause me to hear it. Make haste, my beloved, and be thou like to a roe or to a young hart upon the mountains of spices.'

If we trust the Son of God we are the children of God. In everlasting love the eternal God chose us and adopted us and claimed us as his own beloved sons and daughters (1 John 3:1).

We are redeemed. God's own dear Son, the Lord Jesus Christ, lived in righteousness as our Representative to fulfil all righteousness for us. And he died at Calvary as our Substitute to satisfy the law and justice of God that was against us.

We are born again. God the Holy Spirit has come into our hearts by sovereign and irresistible grace and given us eternal life in Christ. We are believers. Being compelled by grace divine, we trust the Lord Jesus Christ for all our salvation. We trust Christ alone for our eternal acceptance with God (1 Cor. 1:30).

> My hope is built on nothing less
> Than Jesus' blood and righteousness:
> I dare not trust the sweetest frame,
> But wholly lean on Jesus' name.
> On Christ the solid Rock I stand!
> All other ground is sinking sand.

And we are the heirs of God, heirs of eternal glory. Heaven and all its glory is our eternal inheritance. It is our purchased possession. Our Lord Jesus bought eternal glory for us with his blood. It is our predestined portion. Christ has already claimed it in our name, as our forerunner and our great High Priest. The Holy Spirit is that Seal by which we are preserved unto eternal glory.

Why are we here?

Yet, for the present time, we are required to live in this world. Why? If we are the children of God, redeemed, born again, believers in Christ, and the sure heirs of eternal glory, what are we doing here? Why has our Lord left us upon the earth? This passage of Holy Scripture tells us, at least in part, why we are here and what we are to do while we are in this world. It speaks of our responsibilities as believers with regard to our sister, our service, and our Saviour.

Throughout this Song of Love, Christ and his church have confirmed their love to each other. Both have agreed that their love for one another is as strong as death. His love for us is eternal and immutable. And though our love for him is not in anyway such as it ought to be, yet, if it is true, our love for him can never be destroyed. Because our love for Christ is the gift, operation, and work of God's grace in us, it can no more be destroyed than his love for us can be destroyed.

In these last verses we see Christ and his beloved church, like a loving husband and wife, consulting together about their affairs, considering what they are to do. Having laid their hearts together, they now put their heads together, making plans about their relations and their property. In these last few verses, the Song of Love concludes by giving us some very practical instruction about our responsibilities as believers in this world.

Our sister

In verses 8-10 we see Christ our Lord giving us instruction concerning our responsibility toward our sister. The passage begins with a question of compassion and concern. 'We have a little sister, and she hath no breasts: what shall we do for our sister in the day when she shall be spoken for?' (v. 8). The bride, the church, raises a question of concern about her young, little sister. 'What shall we do for her?' She is saying, 'How can I be of help to my little sister?' Who is this 'little sister' about whom she is so concerned?

It is suggested by John Gill (I think rightly) that this passage speaks prophetically of the church of God scattered among the nations of the Gentile world. Though the gospel was revealed only to the Jews in the Old Testament, the Lord God had espoused a people to himself from the nations of the world before time began. It was plainly revealed in the Old Testament that the barren and desolate Gentiles would be united to the Lord as a bride, and that the church would be made up of both Jews and Gentiles (Isa. 54:1; Hos. 1:10; Rom. 9:25-26).

Here the church of God among the Gentiles is called 'a little sister', because Jewish believers and Gentile believers are children of the same Father. They are called 'little' because they had not yet been honoured with the revelation of God. During the Old Testament age the Gentiles had no breasts, no Scriptures, no prophets, no covenant, no ordinances, no promises, no breasts of consolation and instruction. Though chosen of God, their election was not yet manifest and revealed. But now in Christ both Jew and Gentile are one (Eph. 2:11-13).

Taking the text in its wider range, it is to be applied to all those who belong to the election of grace, who have not yet been called to life in Christ, who have not yet been given faith in him. All of God's elect belong to Christ already. Though they have not yet been courted by him and won to him, those unbelievers who are chosen of God are already his, espoused to him in covenant love; and he will have them (John 10:16; Acts 18:10).

They are our sisters according to the election of grace. They have no breasts (Ezek. 16:7). They have no affection for Christ. They have no principle of grace. They have not yet been spoken for. But the day will come when they shall be spoken for, when the chosen shall be called.

This is the thing for which we labour. By the Spirit of God, through the preaching of the gospel, each of God's elect shall be courted and their hearts shall be won by the Lord Jesus Christ. His love and grace will prevail over their stubborn hearts (Ps. 65:4; 110:3). A blessed day that will be, a day of divine visitation! Does your heart's experience cry, 'Amen! It is so!'

What shall we do for our sister in that day? Those who through grace have been brought to Christ should do what they can to bring others to him. This is the design of the gospel. Let us do what we can to seek our sisters who are chosen and redeemed by Christ. Let us do all things for the elect's sake (2 Tim. 2:10). Use every means and opportunity at our disposal to preach the gospel to them. Pray for them. Earnestly persuade them to consent to Christ and be converted.

In verse 9, our Lord quietens the hearts of his people by assuring us of what he will do for his elect people. 'If she be a wall, we will build upon her a palace of silver: and if she be a door, we will enclose her with boards of cedar.' He says, 'We, my Father, my Spirit, and I will gather our elect ones and we will save them.' It is as though our Lord is saying, 'Let me alone, I will do all that is necessary to be done for my own. Trust me.' He will build his church (Matt. 16:18). He will protect his church. The gates of hell will never prevail against it. And he will perfect his church (Eph. 5:25-27). We must labour faithfully; but the work of salvation is the work of the Lord.

Then in verse 10, the bride acknowledges his favour, his grace, and his faithfulness. 'I am a wall, and my breasts like towers: then was I in his eyes as one that found favour.' Having experienced his saving grace, she willingly trusts him with her little sister. She remembers with fondness the work of God upon her, and knows that what the Lord has done for her he will do for all his chosen ones.

Let us acknowledge that salvation is altogether the work of God (Ex. 14:13). It is entirely a matter of divine favour. 'Then was I in his eyes as one that found favour.' Let us trust the Lord to save his people. We have every reason to do so. We have every reason to be confident concerning the salvation of God's elect. His purpose cannot be defeated. Christ's blood cannot be shed in vain. God's grace cannot be frustrated. His power cannot be resisted. His chosen people cannot perish.

Our service

In verses 11-12, we have a word of instruction regarding the responsibilities we have in our service for Christ. 'Solomon had a vineyard at Baalhamon; he let out the vineyard unto keepers; every one for the fruit thereof was to bring a thousand pieces of silver. My vineyard, which is mine, is before me: thou, O Solomon, must have a thousand, and those that keep the fruit thereof two hundred.'

Here the bride consults with Christ about a vineyard they had in the country. – 'Solomon had a vineyard in Baalhamon.' As Solomon was a type of Christ, so his vineyard is a type of the church of Christ (See Matt. 21:33).

The church is Christ's vineyard. The Lord has entrusted each of us with his vineyard, as keepers of it. Though this is primarily the work of faithful pastors, every believer is also entrusted with a part of the work in the vineyard. The service of the church is to be our business in this world; each according to the capacity God has given us. Our Saviour's cause must be our cause.

The Lord expects rent from those that are employed in his vineyard and entrusted with it. What will you do for Christ? What will you do for the increase of his kingdom? What will you do for the furtherance of his gospel? Each of us must serve the interests of his kingdom in this world, for the honour and glory of our Redeemer. The best way to honour Christ is to serve Christ in the place where you are.

While every believer must keep the vineyard of his own heart for Christ (S. of S. 1:6), as we endeavour to serve our Lord, being motivated only by love for him and zeal for his glory, we shall enrich our own souls. 'Those that keep the fruit thereof two hundred.' As Matthew Henry put it, 'Those that work for Christ are working for themselves, and shall be unspeakable gainers by it' (See 2 Cor. 9:6; Gal. 6:6-8).

Our Saviour

The last word in this Song of Love has to do with our responsibility toward our Saviour. 'Thou that dwellest in the gardens, the companions hearken to thy voice: cause me to hear it. Make haste, my beloved, and be thou like to a roe or to a young hart upon the mountains of spices.'

Here we see a picture of Christ and his bride as they must for a while be separated. She must stay below in the gardens on earth, where she has a work to do for him. He must ascend to the mountains of spices in heaven, where he has a work to do for her as an Advocate with the Father.

Our Lord lets us know that he desires to hear from us often. He says, 'Cause me to hear' (v. 13). He is saying, 'My beloved children, cause me to hear your voice. Speak as freely to me as you do to one another. Bring your cares, your burdens, your needs to me.

Pour your hearts out to me' (Heb. 4:16). Our Lord, not only hears and answers our prayers, he even courts them.

For her part, the bride, the church, the believing heart longs for his speedy return (v. 14). It is good to be here, dwelling among the gardens of our Lord, labouring in his vineyard; but to depart and be with him is far better. Our Lord is coming again (John 14:1-3). It is our business to work and to live in anticipation of his speedy return (1 Thess. 5:6-10).

The comfort and satisfaction we enjoy in communion with Christ inspires in us a longing for his immediate presence. The clusters of grapes that we find in this wilderness should make us long for the full vintage of Canaan. If a day in his courts is sweet, what will an eternity within the veil be! Let us ever remind ourselves, 'Behold, he cometh!' When you arise in the morning, say to yourself, 'Behold, he cometh!' When you lay down at night, say to yourself, 'Behold, he cometh!' As we conclude each day of worship, let us do so in hope and expectation. A better day of worship is coming. An everlasting sabbath shall soon be brought in.

We must perhaps remain here for a while. While we are here we have something to do. Let us give ourselves whole-heartedly to the work. We have yet some of our sisters who must be sought. We have our service to perform for the good of the church, for the glory and honour of our Redeemer. We have our Saviour to watch for in prayer and faith. He says, 'Surely, I come quickly.' And our hearts respond, 'Amen. Even so, come, Lord Jesus.'

30.

Our Lord's vineyard

Song of Solomon 8:12

'My vineyard, which is mine, is before me: thou, O Solomon, must have a thousand, and those that keep the fruit thereof two hundred.'

The Song of Solomon is really a series of responsive songs. It must be read and understood spiritually. This poetic book is a symbolical picture of Christ and his church. Wherever we see Solomon speaking, it is Christ speaking to his church. Wherever we see the Shulamite speaking to her Beloved, it is the church speaking to Christ. Throughout this 'Song of Songs' we hear Christ speaking to us, his church, his bride, his spouse; and then the church responds to his words of love in tones of sincere affection and admiration.

The very fact that this is a responsive song makes it at times difficult to understand, because it is not always easy to determine who is speaking in a given passage — Christ or his church. For example, the commentators are just about equally divided over this sentence: 'My vineyard, which is mine, is before me.' Some say, 'This is Christ speaking to his church.' Others insist, 'This is the church speaking to Christ.'

Personally, I cannot say. I cannot press the issue one way, or the other. So I will take this sentence ('My vineyard, which is mine, is before me.') as coming from the lips of our Lord to his church. Then view it as coming from the bride. I believe that our souls will be greatly profited by both considerations.

The church

The vineyard spoken of in this text is the church of Christ (Ps. 80:8-10, 14-15). The church is the vineyard of our Lord Jesus Christ, always under his watchful eye and tender care. I use the word 'church' here in reference to the church universal, the mystical, spiritual body of Christ. The church is the whole body of God's elect, the whole family of God. All true believers of every age are in the church. We are all one body in Christ, who is our Head (1 Cor. 12:13; Eph. 2:13-14).

Other trees may be useful for lumber or firewood, though they bring forth no fruit. But a vine is only useful when it is fruitful. If a vine is fruitless it is useless. It cumbers the ground. It must be cut down and burned. The church is frequently compared to a vine, or vineyard, in the Scriptures (Isa. 5:1, 2, 7; John 15:1-10). It is compared to a vine because of its fruitfulness and because as a vine, which has many branches, is one, even so the church of Christ is one body in Christ, though it has many members.

'My vineyard'

'My vineyard, which is mine, is before me.' With these words, our Lord Jesus Christ claims the church as his own and declares his special love and care for it. The Lord here declares that the church is his own special property. He makes the claim twice, 'My vineyard, which is mine.' He declares his rights of ownership. He looks upon his church, his believing people, those whom he has chosen and redeemed, and says, 'This is my vineyard.'

We know that all things belong to our Lord Jesus Christ (Rev. 4:11). All things are his by right of creation. All things are his by the prerogative of providence. And all things are his by virtue of his mediatorial reign (John 17:2). But our Lord here claims a special interest in and possession of his church.

It is true that our Lord is providentially good and benevolent to all his creatures. But the special object of our Saviour's love, care, and concern is his own vineyard, his church. In providence he rules over all things and all people; but the object, goal, and purpose of his rule is the welfare of his church (John 17:2; Rom. 8:28).

The church belongs to Christ by divine gift from his Father (John 17:6, 9, 11, 12). The church is the property of all the three persons of the Holy Trinity. She belongs to God the Father by eternal election. She belongs to God the Son by donation, by Suretyship agreement. And she belongs to God the Holy Spirit by his indwelling presence and special habitation (Eph. 2:20-22).

The church belongs to Christ by a lawful purchase (Acts 20:28; Eph. 5:25-27). There are some who say that all men were purchased by Christ. But God's people do not believe in such sham redemption, a redemption that does not redeem. We do not believe in a universal atonement, which extends even to those who were in hell before Christ died. Such an atonement is no atonement at all. We believe in an effectual redemption, a particular and special atonement. We can never tolerate the doctrine of those who would tell us that Christ died in vain, and that some of those for whom he died will perish in hell. Our Lord will never part with his church. He will never lose one of his redeemed ones. He paid too dear a price for us.

The church belongs to Christ as a bride belongs to her husband (Hos. 2:14-3:3). He chose us as the object of his love. He redeemed us with his own precious blood. He has courted us, wooed our hearts, and won our love by his gracious Spirit. He will not allow us to be lost. He will never leave us. He will never allow us to leave him.

Constant care

The church is the special property of Christ. He says, 'My vineyard, which is mine.' But there is more. In this sentence, our Lord also declares that his church is the constant object of his watchful eye and special care — 'My vineyard, which is mine, is before me.' Those words, as coming from the lips of Christ, are full of meaning for the comfort of our hearts — 'My vineyard is before me.' He is saying to us, 'Fear not, my eye is upon you. I am engaged to do you good.' (See Isa. 41:10, 14).

The church is before Christ in the sense that he so loves us that he will never let us out of his presence. The vineyard is so dear to him that he never leaves it. He may sometimes hide himself among the vines; but he is always present (Matt. 28:20; Heb. 13:5). He still walks among the golden candlesticks. This statement by our Lord also means that he is always caring for his church. His providence is constantly engaged for our everlasting good. He has done us good. He is doing us good. And he will do us good. All things work together for our good.

In this expression there is also the assurance that the Lord is knowledgeable of his church. He knows us. He is thoroughly acquainted with us and with all that concerns us. There is a sweet thought here for all who love Christ. You as his church, each one of his people are especially preserved by Christ. We are personally, particularly, distinctly, and eternally the objects of his love and care.

Let us ever remember, the church is the Lord's own vineyard. He will take care of her. He will maintain her cause. He will provide her needs. He will build her walls, establish her gates, and secure her success. The church does not belong to the pastor, or to the people, but to Christ alone. The church belongs to Christ. We are under his care.

The keepers

Now read verses 11 and 12 together. 'Solomon had a vineyard at Baalhamon; he let out the vineyard unto keepers; every one for the fruit thereof was to bring a thousand pieces of silver. My vineyard, which is mine, is before me: thou, O Solomon, must have a thousand, and those that keep the fruit thereof two hundred.'

In verse 11 several things are set before us. As we have seen, the church of God in this world is Christ's vineyard. The Lord Jesus has trusted the care of his vineyard to chosen men (Matt. 20:1-2; 21:33). Gospel preachers are the Lord's rent-gatherers. They collect his fruit and bring it in to him (John 15:16). The fruit gathered and brought by these keepers of the Lord's vineyard is all the same.

The fruit brought in by each one is 'a thousand pieces of silver.' God's servants all have the same commission to preach the gospel. They have different gifts and abilities. And their outward, apparent successes differ. Some have greater and some lesser success, at least in their own eyes and in the eyes of men. 'Yet,' as John Gill wrote, 'in the faithful and honest discharge of their work, they are all so blessed by him, as to answer the end of their ministration (ministry) designed by him; so that he reckons that every one, even the meanest (most humble and least gifted), brings in his thousand pieces, as well as the more able and successful.'

Our responsibility

Now, read this sentence as though it were spoken by the church, as spoken by us to our Saviour — 'My vineyard, which is mine, is before me.' This is the language of the church about her responsibility to Christ, the Lord. The church is Christ's vineyard. It belongs to him. But he has let his vineyard out to many 'keepers' (v. 11). It is our responsibility, as 'keepers' of the vineyard, to be faithful stewards over that which the Lord has committed to our care.

The care of Christ's vineyard is not the responsibility of God's appointed pastors alone. We are each responsible for the Lord's vineyard. Every believer is responsible for his own heart, his own life, and his own work (S. of S. 1:6). If you are a believer, if you are one of those men or women who belong to Christ, you are a 'keeper' of the Lord's vineyard. He has placed into your hands, under your care, a part of that vineyard which is so dear to him that he paid for it with his own life's blood. Now, it is your responsibility to faithfully serve him in his vineyard. Keep your heart for him (Prov. 4:23). Keep your life for him. See that your life upon this earth is a life lived for the honour and glory of Christ (Col. 3:1-3).

Let us learn the lesson he taught Peter in John 21:20-21. Let us faithfully keep to the work that he has given us. Serve the Lord where you are. To serve him is to serve his people and to serve his cause. We are not all called to preach the gospel; but there is something that each of us can do, something we are responsible to do, something that we must do for Christ, for the good of his church, for the furtherance of his gospel. We can all visit his sick and afflicted people, and comfort them in their trouble. We can all bear faithful witness of Christ. We can all bring people to hear the gospel. We can all minister to the needs of God's servants. We can all mow grass, rake leaves, wash windows, paint, dust and keep the doors of the Lord's house (take care of the church property), making a comfortable place for people to hear the gospel and worship our God. We can all give generously to the support of the ministry. We can all look for and seize every opportunity to express and show our love to God's saints, comforting the hurting, forgiving the offensive, restoring the fallen, and encouraging the weak. We can all do much for the furtherance of the gospel. And what we can do, what God gives us the means, opportunity, and ability to do we must do for the glory of Christ and the good of his people.

There are some who are given special talents and special responsibilities as 'keepers' in the Lord's vineyard. With special talents come special responsibilities. I am given the privilege and the awesome responsibility of being one of the Lord's pastors, an under-shepherd, a keeper of the Lord's vineyard. Others are missionaries, evangelists, elders or teachers. Others are deacons. There is one thing, only one thing that our God requires of us in each of our respective places. That one thing is faithfulness (1 Cor. 4:1-2).

As a steward under God, whatever the work is God has given us, let us say, 'This is my vineyard. It is the vineyard God has given to me. This is the sphere and place of my responsibility. This is the portion of the wall I must build. It is before me.' I am not responsible for my brother's work; but I am responsible for my own. I must always keep my own work before my eyes. I must go about my work, doing what I have to do, just as though there were no one else in the world to do anything.

If I see another man prospering more than me, I will thank God for his blessing upon my brother and his work. But still I must say, 'My vineyard, which is mine, is before me.' I do not look for, nor do I desire another man's place. This is the place God has for me. This is the work God has committed to my hands. This is the place where I must faithfully serve him.

What about you? Will you be faithful in the place where the Lord has put you, and faithful in the work he has set before you?

The fruit

'Thou, O Solomon, must have a thousand, and those that keep the fruit thereof two hundred.' This is the declaration of the church to her great Lord. The fruit of the vineyard belongs to Christ and he must have it. Jesus Christ must have the fruit of his vineyard. That is to say, he must receive all the honour, all the glory, and all the praise from his church. We must not applaud ourselves if God's blessings attend our labours. We must not exalt and magnify those who labour most zealously and those who give most generously. We must not give glory and praise to those faithful pastors, teaches, missionaries, etc. through whom the Lord speaks and works. There is no place in the church of God for the honour of the flesh. 'He that glorieth, let him glory in the Lord.' No flesh shall glory in his presence.

The keepers of the vineyard shall receive their reward as well. There is no promise here of heavenly rewards and crowns being earned by faithful service to Christ. But this fact must not be ignored: Those who honour God, God will honour (1 Sam. 2:30). Each man and woman who faithfully serves the Lord Jesus Christ will find great reward in doing so. Your own soul will be profited by your faithfulness. And such men and women should be highly esteemed by those who profit by their labours. Those who are faithful missionaries, pastors, teachers, elders, and deacons in the church should be given their proper respect and esteem.

Those who preach the gospel of Christ are to be rewarded for their labours by those for whom they labour. Every true and faithful servant of God is to be esteemed very highly for his work's sake (1 Thess. 5:12-13). One of the old writers made this observation: 'Where Christ gets his due among a people, there and there only do ministers get their due. Where Christ is heartily received, the feet of them that bring glad tidings will be beautiful. Where Christ has his thousand, ministers will have their two hundred.' Those who preach the gospel are to live by the gospel. They are to be generously supported and maintained by their congregations (1 Tim. 5:17-18; Gal. 6:6; 1 Cor. 9:9-11).

This two hundred, which is the reward of God's servants, certainly includes those chosen, redeemed sinners who are converted by the Spirit of God under their influence (1 Thess. 2:19-20). This two hundred shall be the full possession and compensation of every servant of God in eternal glory. Here, we may seem to come far short of it. Poverty, disrespect, and reproach are the common lot of faithful gospel preachers in this world. But there is a day coming when 'they that turn many to righteousness shall shine as the stars for ever and ever' (Dan. 12:3; 2 Tim. 4:6-8).

The church belongs to Christ. It is his vineyard, always under his watchful eye and the object of his loving care. It is our responsibility to faithfully serve the Lord Jesus Christ in the place where we are, with the capacity he has given us. Those who faithfully serve Christ, all of them, are to be duly honoured by us.

31.

The Lord's last Word to his church

Song of Solomon 8:13

'Thou that dwellest in the gardens, the companions hearken to thy voice: cause me to hear it.'

Nothing is more precious in the memory of a woman whose beloved husband has gone to be with the Lord than her dear husband's last words to her. How often I have sat across the room from a widow, whose husband had departed many years before, and heard her say, 'I can remember the last thing he said to me, as though it were just yesterday.' The last words spoken by a loving companion are precious words. Even so, the last words of our Lord Jesus Christ to his believing people are words we particularly, tenderly cherish in our hearts (John 14 -17).

The Song of Songs is almost ended. The chosen bride and the Glorious Bridegroom have come to their last stanzas. They are about to part company for a while. The Lord, our Saviour, our Great Bridegroom must depart this world for a season. His bodily presence must be taken from us. He must enter again into his glory. And his bride, the church, which he has chosen and redeemed with his own precious blood, must remain upon the earth until he comes for her. Therefore, the Bridegroom, our Lord Jesus Christ, bids us farewell. These are the last words of our Saviour to his believing people. 'Thou that dwellest in the gardens, the companions hearken to thy voice: cause me to hear it.'

In other words, our Lord says to each of us — While I am away from you, fill this garden with my name, and let your heart commune with me. As she sees him rising up into the clouds of glory, the bride quickly responds — 'Make haste, my beloved, and be thou like to a roe or to a young hart upon the mountains of spices.' It is as though she said — I know, my Love, that you must go away for a while; but hurry back. As soon as it pleases you, when my work upon the earth is done, come to me again; and take me home to the ivory palaces of glory land.

Expedient

Even his leaving us was an act of great love and grace. In fact, it was his greatest act of love. If he had not left us and gone to the tree of his death and up to the throne of glory, we could never have been redeemed and saved, we could never have entered into glory. He said, 'I tell you the truth: It is expedient for you that I go away: for if I go not away, the Comforter will not come unto you; but if I depart, I will send him unto you' (John 16:7).

It was truly expedient for our Lord to go away, to suffer, die, rise again, and ascend into glory. By his going away to die for us and to live again for us in heaven, many evils were prevented from falling upon us, which otherwise would have destroyed us. He went away to save us from the heavy strokes of divine justice, the wrath, vengeance, curse, and condemnation of God's holy law, the eternal ruin, misery and death of hell.

Our Lord's going away was expedient for us, because he went away to obtain for us all the blessings of grace and eternal good for our souls: redemption — reconciliation — forgiveness — righteousness — eternal life — peace — heavenly glory. When we realize what the Lord Jesus Christ has done for us, we know that it is best for us that he went away for a while. He has opened for us an entrance into the holiest by the blood of his cross (Heb. 10:19-

22). He has taken possession of heaven and eternal glory as our Representative (Heb. 6:20). He has gone to prepare a place for us in glory, in the Father's house (John 14:1-3). He has gone away to appear in the presence of God for us (1 John 2:1-2). He has gone away so that he might send his promised Spirit into the world to gather his elect from the four corners of the earth, to regenerate, sanctify, and preserve them unto his eternal glory (Gal. 3:13-14).

Truly, it is best for us that our beloved Saviour has gone away. Surely, then the last words of our heavenly Bridegroom must be of special interest to us. 'Thou that dwellest in the gardens, the companions hearken to thy voice: cause me to hear it.' With those parting words, our blessed Saviour tells us most plainly what he desires of us while we are yet upon this earth.

Our dwelling place

First, our Lord describes his bride as one who enjoys the benefits of a blessed residence. 'Thou that dwellest in the gardens.' The Hebrew construction of this phrase is in the feminine. Literally, the Lord is calling his bride, his church, by this name, 'Thou inhabitress of the gardens.' We who are born of God, we who make up the church of Christ, the body of God's elect are addressed under this term — 'Thou inhabitress of the gardens.' It describes our residence upon the earth, the assembly of God's saints, the congregation of the Lord.

This term distinguishes us from our Lord. He whom we love dwells in the ivory palaces. He has gone up to his Father's throne. But he has left us in these gardens here below. He dwelt here with us for a while. But now he has finished the work that his Father gave him to do and he has returned to his throne. He is no longer physically present with us. Our Lord's presence with his church is real, true, and constant; but it is a spiritual, rather than physical presence, that we now enjoy (Matt. 18:20; John 14:23).

Like our Saviour, we must remain upon the earth, dwelling in his gardens, until our work upon the earth is done (John 14:12).

Our Lord has gone to heaven, because he best accomplishes the purposes of God from there. He has left us upon the earth to serve him, because we best accomplish the purpose of God here.

Our place is in the King's gardens. This is the place of our great employment. Those who serve the Lord serve him by serving his garden, the local church, the assembly of his people. Each of God's people is placed in the garden for the good of his own soul and for the service of the Lord's church. 'You and I are set in the garden of the church, because there is a work for us to do which will be beneficial to others and to ourselves also' (C. H. Spurgeon). It is best for us, for the glory of God and for the church of Christ that we abide here a while longer. Here 'ye are the lights of the world'. Here 'ye are the salt of the earth'. Here you abide as dew from the Lord in this dry and thirsty land. Have you found out what it is the Lord has for you to do in his gardens? Have you found the tender plants for which you are to care?

This is the place of our great enjoyment. This is the place where the Lord meets with us, instructs us, teaches us, refreshes us, and makes himself known to us (S. of S. 6:2). I cannot overstress the importance of the local assembly of God's saints in the life of a believer (Heb. 10:26). The Lord himself walks in his garden. The River of the Water of Life flows through the garden. The Tree of Life is planted in the Lord's garden.

This is the place of our great eminence. The greatest blessing God can ever give to you or me upon this earth is the privilege of dwelling in one of the Lord's gardens. The greatest blessing God ever gave to a community of men is the establishment of a local church where the gospel is preached. And the greatest curse God ever sent to any place was withdrawing from them the witness of a gospel church.

This is the place of our great establishment. 'Thou that dwellest'. These words imply a permanent residence, a permanent establishment. As for me and my house, we are established in the house of God, the garden of the Lord. All things are secondary to this. I am ready to give up anything before I will give up the worship of God, the fellowship of his saints, and the ministry of the Word.

> How charming is the place
> Where my Redeemer God
> Unveils the beauties of his face,
> And sheds his love abroad.

> Not all the fair palaces,
> To which the great resort,
> Are once to be compared with this,
> Where Jesus holds his court.

There is nothing more important to a believer than the blessed residence God has appointed for his people, the Garden of the Lord, the Church of God, the House of Prayer. I leave it to you to judge whether or not you have found the Church of God a garden for your soul and this garden a blessed residence in which to dwell.

> I love thy church, O God!
> Her walls before thee stand,
> Dear as the apple of thine eye
> And graven on thy hand.

> For her my tears shall fall,
> For her my prayers ascend —
> To her my cares and toils be given
> Till cares and toils shall end.

Our family

Second, our Lord speaks of the relationship which the people of God should enjoy with one another. 'Thou that dwellest in the gardens, the companions hearken to thy voice.' The church of God is a family. A local assembly, if it is what it should be, is a commune of pilgrims, companions whose hearts and lives are wed to one another. The church of God is his family (Matt. 12:48-50). We will be wise to make it ours.

Let us endeavour to maintain the unity, peace, and joy of our family (Eph. 4:3-7). One thing is essential to every family is communication. Families that get along well must talk to one another. They must know one another, encourage one another, and support one another. This blessed communication between believers is what our Lord is talking about — 'The companions hearken to thy voice!' Build your relationships with God's people by personal conversation and pleasant communion. Like marriages, good relationships with other people do not just happen; they must be built.

Heaven will, in great measure, be an everlasting communion of saints. If we would enjoy heaven below we must commune with one another. Be sure that your conversations with others are edifying, Christ honouring, and spiritually beneficial. I do not mean that you must always talk to others about spiritual things; but I do mean that you should strive to be spiritually helpful to one another in your speech. When we come together in the house of God, we should be especially careful to assist one another in our conversations before the service and after the service. Be careful to maintain and display real, genuine interest in others. Many appear to be afraid to speak any word of praise, congratulations, or honour to another. Yet, our God tells us to give honour to those to whom honour is due. And none are more worthily honoured by us than those who serve the Lord with us. Truthful and thoughtful commendation is never out of order.

Communion with Christ

Third, our Lord makes a great, tender, condescending request of us. It is a request that will prove to be for our souls' good. May he give us grace ever to heed it. 'Thou that dwellest in the gardens,

the companions hearken to thy voice: cause me to hear it.' It is as
though our Lord were saying to us — 'I am going away for a while,
and you will see me no more; but I will not forget you. My heart
will always be with you. Therefore, do not forget me. Cause me
to hear your voice. Though you cannot see me with your physical
eye, nor audibly hear my voice, I can see you and hear you. So
cause me to hear your voice.'

This is a very natural request. Love seeks the company of
its object. It is a request that seems to have many implications.
Our Saviour seems to be saying, 'Cause me to hear your voice in
prayer, in praise, in intimate communion. Cause me to hear the
voice of your heart.' Our ever-gracious Christ desires to hear the
inmost groans and sighs and feelings of our hearts, as well as the
joy and laughter of our hearts (Heb. 4:16; Phil. 4:6-7; 1 Pet. 5:6-
7). He says, 'Cause me to hear your voice frequently, reverently, in
faith and honesty. Cause me to hear your voice.'

Our responsibility

There is one more thing hidden in our text. The text could be translated like this, 'Thou that dwellest in the gardens, the companions
hearken to thy voice: Cause them to hear me.' Read this way, our
Saviour is saying, 'Since you are among them, and they hear your
voice, be sure that you cause them to hear of me. Make those who
dwell in the garden with you hear your voice speaking of me.'

We should often speak to one another, and to those strangers who happen to come into the house of worship, and to those
we meet in the streets, of Christ. The Lord has given us the gift of
speech; we should use it to tell of him. Cause Christ to be heard.
Use your voice to speak of his glorious person, of his wondrous
works, and his amazing, saving, bounteous grace.

32.

Come, my beloved

Song of Solomon 8:14

'*Make haste, my beloved, and be thou like to a roe or to a young hart upon the mountains of spices.*'

The Song of Solomon is an allegorical song that describes the love of Christ for his people and the love of all believing hearts for the Lord Jesus Christ. Our Lord's last word to his church in this Song of Love was that he might often hear her voice. 'Thou that dwellest in the gardens, the companions hearken to thy voice: cause me to hear it.'

But the last verse of the song comes from the heart of his bride upon the earth. It expresses the intense desire of every believing heart in this world and the great longing of God's church that the Lord Jesus Christ, who has gone into heaven, should return again. This last verse of the song is a prayer for our Saviour's glorious second advent. 'Make haste, my beloved, and be thou like to a roe or to a young hart upon the mountains of spices.'

This is very much like the prayer John recorded at the close of the Book of Revelation — 'Even so, come, Lord Jesus.' You promised, when you went away to prepare a place for us, that you would come and receive us unto yourself, that we might forever dwell in your presence. Our hearts are filled with hope. We look for you. We wait for you. We long for you. Even now we pray, 'Come, my beloved.'

Is this your heart's desire? Do you long for the Lord's glorious advent? Do you desire his speedy return? Are you looking for his appearing? I am afraid that far too often we accept the doctrine of the second coming in our heads, but have no real desire for it in our hearts. As we conclude our study of this blessed Song, I want to do what I can to stir up that blessed hope that is within us. May God the Holy Spirit arouse in you and me an earnest desire for and anticipation of our Lord's second advent. We who believe should live everyday upon the tiptoe of faith, anticipating our Lord's second coming. We look for no signs. We set no dates. But we are to look for Christ, as it were, upon the very tiptoe of expectant faith.

The Beloved

First, I call your attention to the fact that the Lord Jesus Christ is the beloved object of believing hearts. Here is the title his bride gives him — 'My beloved'. True religion has many sides. True religion is practical. True religion is doctrinal. And true religion is personal. But it matters not how practical, doctrinal, and personal our religion is, if our religion does not produce in us a genuine love for Christ our religion is not true. All of God's people love Christ. We do not love him as we should. We do not love him as we would. And we do not love him as we shall. But we do love the Son of God. He is the Beloved of our hearts (1 Cor. 16:22; 1 Pet. 2:7).

This is the true testimony of all believers, 'We love him, because he first loved us' (1 John 4:19). We do not love him as we should. Our love for Christ is not in anyway worthy of his love for us; but we do love him. He loved us before we loved him (Jer. 31:3). He loves us infinitely superior to our love for him (1 John 3:16; 4:9-10). And his love for us is the cause of our love for him. 'We love him, because he first loved us.' But if we are true believers we do truly love the Lord Jesus Christ.

We love him sincerely, love him supremely, and love him grow-ingly. We love him, because of who he is. And we love him, be-cause of what he has done. Where there is true faith in the heart, there is genuine, sincere, increasing love for the Lord Jesus Christ (Luke 14:25-27, 33). We may be reluctant to sing the words of the hymn, ashamed because our love for our Redeemer is so inde-scribably unworthy of him; but every child of God can sing with A. J. Gordon, and can do so honestly…

My Jesus, I love thee, I know thou art mine,
For thee all the follies of sin I resign;
My gracious Redeemer, my Saviour art thou;
If ever I loved thee, my Jesus, 'tis now.

I love thee, because thou hast first loved me,
And purchased my pardon on Calvary's tree;
I love thee for wearing the thorns on thy brow;
If ever I loved thee, my Jesus 'tis now.

I'll love thee in life, I will love thee in death,
And praise thee as long as thou lendest me breath;
And say when the death dew lies cold on my brow,
If ever I loved thee, my Jesus, 'tis now.

In mansions of glory and endless delight,
I'll ever adore thee in heaven so bright;
I'll sing as I'm casting the crown from my brow;
If ever I loved thee, my Jesus, 'tis now.

Believers are people whose lives are ruled, governed, and mo-tivated by the love of Christ (2 Cor. 5:14). It is not our love for him that is the proof of his love for us. The proof of his love for us is our faith in him (Heb. 11:1). But the fruit of faith in Christ is love for Christ. It is written, 'Unto you therefore which believe he is pre-cious' (1 Pet. 2:7).

Upon the mountains

Second, the Lord Jesus, our Beloved, is to be seen upon the mountains of spices. 'Make haste, my beloved, and be thou like to a roe or to a young hart upon the mountains of spices.' What does this mean? She is calling for him to come from the place where he now is, 'the mountains of spices'. As we have gone through the Song of Solomon, we have seen four references to mountains.

'The Mountains of Bether' (2:17) — Bether means 'divisions'. There was standing between us and our God three great mountains of divisions (God's righteousness, his justice, and our sins) that separated us from him. We could never cross over them to God, but our divine Saviour crossed over them and reconciled us to God. Christ our Mediator has levelled these mountains of division.

'The Mountains of Leopards' (4:8) — Like dark mountains filled with leopards, sin, death, hell, and Satan terrified our souls. The Lord Jesus, our Beloved, the mighty Conqueror has overcome these.

'The Mountain of Myrrh' (4:6) — Myrrh is both bitter and fragrant. Oh, what bitterness our Beloved endured that he might be for us a sweet-smelling savour to God! When the Lord of Glory, the Son of God who knew no sin, was made to be sin for us, he was forsaken by his Father! His Father, at the very height of his obedience to him, abandoned him! But more, all the just anger, wrath, and fury of the Almighty against sin was poured out upon him to the full satisfaction of divine justice! Willingly, because of his love for us, Immanuel drank the cup of bitterness, until the last bitter dregs of divine indignation were gone! It was all bitterness to him; but his sin-atoning sacrifice is sweet fragrance to God for us (Eph. 5:1-2).

'The Mountains of Spices' (8:14) — The mountains of spices are the mountains of heaven itself where our Redeemer dwells today. He sits as King upon his holy hill in Mt Zion. John Gill wrote, 'The joys and glories of the heavenly state are here intended; where the church desires to have everlasting and uninterrupted communion with her Beloved, and that speedily, if it was his will; where she should be on high, and out of the reach of every snare and every enemy; where she would be safe, secure and immoveable, and in the possession of pleasures that will never end.'

He continues, 'These mountains may denote the height and sublimity of this happy state. It is above. It is an 'inheritance reserved in heaven; a hope laid up there, a prize of the high calling of God in Christ Jesus'. They may express the permanence and everlastingness thereof. It is a 'city which hath foundations', and these immoveable. It is a 'building of God, eternal in the heavens.' These habitations are everlasting, from whence there never will be a remove. They may signify the exceeding pleasantness and delightfulness thereof: that state may well be represented by' spicy mountains, seeing in the presence of Christ there 'is fullness of joy, and at his right hand there are pleasures for evermore'. No wonder, then, that the church should so passionately wish for the enjoyment of this happiness; and close this song in the manner she does, saying, 'Make haste, my beloved, and be thou like a roe or a young hart upon the mountains of spices.'

What are the spices of the high, immoveable mountains of heavenly glory? The spices cannot be anything other than the merits and efficacy of Christ's blood and righteousness and intercession for his own, and his everlasting praise as our all-glorious Redeemer, Saviour and God.

The prayer

Every believing heart should desire and anticipate the coming of Christ, ever crying, 'Make haste, my beloved.'

> For the grace of God that bringeth salvation hath appeared to all men, Teaching us that, denying ungodliness and worldly lusts, we should live soberly, righteously, and godly, in this present world; Looking for that blessed hope, and the glorious appearing of the great God and our Sav-

iour Jesus Christ; Who gave himself for us, that he might redeem us from all iniquity, and purify unto himself a peculiar people, zealous of good works.

Seeing then that all these things shall be dissolved, what manner of persons ought ye to be in all holy conversation and godliness, Looking for and hasting unto the coming of the day of God, wherein the heavens being on fire shall be dissolved, and the elements shall melt with fervent heat? Nevertheless we, according to his promise, look for new heavens and a new earth, wherein dwelleth righteousness. Wherefore, beloved, seeing that ye look for such things, be diligent that ye may be found of him in peace, without spot, and blameless (Tit. 2:11-14; 2 Pet. 3:11-14).

Why should we be so anxious for the speedy return of Christ? Why should we so eagerly anticipate the glorious appearing of the great God and our Saviour, the Lord Jesus Christ? This is the result of true love. A loving wife longs for the return of her husband who has been so long away from her. When our Saviour comes, he will bring an end to all the conflict we now endure. When our Lord comes, there will be a great resurrection, and we shall see his face forever (Job 19:25-27; 1 Thess. 4:13-17). When King Jesus appears in his glory, he will create all things new, and God shall wipe away all tears from our eyes.

When our great God and Saviour comes in power and in great glory, he will sit upon the Great White Throne of Judgement. His is a throne of sovereign power. His is a white throne of absolute purity and judgement. It will be a great day indeed when the great King of Glory sits upon the Throne of Judgement. In that day, he will put all things in order and show all things in their true light. He will clear his own elect of all charges and accusations. He will show the honour of his Name in all that he has done. He will display the glory of his grace in his people. He will tread upon the necks of all his enemies. He will be glorious! 'Behold, he cometh!' 'Every eye shall see him.' What will become of you when you see the Lord Jesus Christ in his glory?

Notes

Chapter 7. 'Winter is past'

1. I am not impressed by most of what has been called revival in church history. That which is commonly called revival appears to me to be more demonic than heavenly. Most would call the events recorded in 1 Kings 18:26, 28, and 29 revival, if they were to occur today and the word Jesus were used instead of Baal. But true revival came in verse 39. When God works his wonders in the midst of his people, he does not cause fleshly, charismatic show of emotional frenzy. Rather, he causes sinners to be awed before him in worship, bowing before the throne of his sovereign majesty (read Isaiah 6, Joel 2 and Acts 2). Whatever revival is, it is not a spasmodic fit of religion, with only temporary results. Rather, it is Christ seizing the hearts of men and women by his omnipotent grace.

Chapter 10. Christ and his church in their royal chariot

1. 1 Kings 11:1 clearly shows that Solomon's choice of Pharaoh's daughter for one of his wives was, on his part, an act of disobedience to God. But that fact does not nullify the typical meaning of this passage. No type of our Savior is full and perfect. Yet, by way of contrast, while it was a shameful thing for Solomon to take Pharaoh's daughter for his wife, it is the glory of Christ to take sinners altogether unfit for his bride to be his bride. Taking such as we are

into union with himself, robed in his righteousness and washed in his blood, we are made perfectly righteous and completely worthy of him.

Chapter 15. **Let me tell you about my Beloved**

1. The name for man, 'Adam', means 'red earth'.

.